Contents

Part 1

Introduction

Shakespeare's life and times

Shakespeare's life

We know that Shakespeare was baptised in Holy Trinity Church at Stratford-upon-Avon on 26 April 1564 and that he was buried there on 25 April 1616, but we know for certain very little more about the life of the greatest English dramatist and poet. Shakespeare's name does appear on some forty official documents and his family is mentioned in many others; he is named occasionally by some of his contemporary dramatists and writers; and, later in the seventeenth century, a good deal of gossip about him was recorded. From these sources we can make out the main lines of his life, but only so far as his public activities are concerned. His inner life, how he thought about his plays, his beliefs, prejudices and the like, these are hidden from us. As a result, many scholars have tried to detect in the plays clues to Shakespeare's character and thoughts, but this is a very difficult thing to do. Shakespeare submerges himself in the characters he creates to a greater extent than any other writer. His ability to imagine and recreate so many different people, with their different emotions and attitudes, means that we can never be sure when we read in the plays Shakespeare's own convictions and when we read simply those sentiments befitting the character who speaks. Shakespeare the man eludes us.

We do know that Shakespeare was born into a well-to-do family in the country market town of Stratford-upon-Avon in Warwickshire. His father, John Shakespeare, was a prosperous trader and merchant and a person of some importance in the town. In 1568 he became high bailiff (or mayor) of Stratford. In 1557 he had married Mary Arden. Their third child and eldest son, William, went to the local grammar school, where he would have studied Latin, history, logic and rhetoric. In November 1582 William, then aged eighteen, married Anne Hathaway, who was twenty-six years old. They had a daughter (Susanna) in May 1583, and twins (Hamnet and Judith) in 1585.

And that is all we can say about Shakespeare until he is mentioned in 1592 in a pamphlet called *A Groatsworth of Wit* by the playwright and romance writer Robert Greene. From this reference we learn that Shakespeare was then an actor and dramatist in London, but when he left Stratford, and why he left, we simply do not know. What he did during these 'lost years' 1585–92 has been much discussed, but nothing has been proved. Robert Greene is cross in his pamphlet because the 'upstart' Shakespeare, of whom he thinks little, is setting himself up as the equal of established London dramatists. To have aroused this hostility from a competitor, Shakespeare must, by 1592, have been long enough in London to have made a name for himself as a dramatist. We may guess, therefore, that he left Stratford in 1586 or 1587, but it is only a guess.

During the next twenty years Shakespeare continued to live in London, perhaps visiting his wife and family in Stratford each year. He continued to act, but his chief fame was as a playwright. His plays were very popular and brought him considerable wealth. He was able to buy lands around Stratford, and a large house in the town, to which he retired in 1611. He died there on 23 April 1616.

The Elizabethan Renaissance

For whatever reason Shakespeare went to London, he could hardly have chosen a better time if he wanted to be a dramatist. This was the beginning of the 'golden age' of English literature, the Elizabethan Renaissance. Although Elizabeth reigned as queen from 1558 to 1603, the term 'Elizabethan' is used very loosely in a literary sense to refer to the period 1580–1625, when the great works of the age were produced. (Some critics distinguish the later part of this period as 'Jacobean' from the name of the king who succeeded Elizabeth, James I, who reigned from 1603 to 1625). The poet Edmund Spenser (1552–99), had heralded the new age with his pastoral poem *The Shepheards Calender* (1579), and his friend Sir Philip Sidney (1554–86) had explained the new theories of poetry in his essay *The Apologie for Poetrie* (written about 1580, although not published until 1595). Spenser's great allegorical epic poem, *The Faerie Queene*, began to appear from 1590, the year in which Sidney's immensely influential prose romance *Arcadia* was published. These two writers established a new set of literary ideals, and a host of other poets strove to imitate them and go beyond what they had accomplished.

But this was not only the great age of poetry. The poetic achievements of the Elizabethans may have been equalled by later poets, but their drama has had no rivals. There had been no theatres during the medieval period and plays were then strictly of a religious nature, performed at Christian festivals by amateur actors. Such professional actors as there were wandered the country, putting on a variety of entertainments in the yards of inns, on make-shift stages in market squares, or anywhere else suitable. They did not perform full length plays, but mimes, juggling and comedy acts. Such actors were generally regarded as little better than vagabonds and layabouts.

Just before Shakespeare went to London all this began to change. A number of young men who had been to the universities of Oxford and Cambridge came to London in the 1580s and began to write plays which made use of what they had learned about the classical drama of ancient Greece and Rome. Plays such as John Lyly's (1553–1606) *Alexander and Campaspe* (1584), Christopher Marlowe's (1564–93) *Tamburlaine the Great* (about 1587), and Thomas Kyd's (1557–95) *The Spanish Tragedy* (1588–9), were unlike anything that had been written in English before. These dramatists and their fellow 'university wits', as they are called, brough a new life, vigour and sophistication to English drama. With the exception of Lyly, who wrote in prose, they wrote in blank verse, not rhymed verse like the old religious drama, and so had greater freedom of expression. They adopted many of the conventions of the classical drama and they wrote on subjects that were not religious, so opening up all history and legend as suitable matter for plays.

The main change, however, was that these playwrights wrote for the professional theatres. In 1576 James Burbage built the first permanent theatre in England just outside London. It was called simply 'The Theatre'. Others soon followed. Thus, when Shakespeare came to London, there was a flourishing drama, theatres and companies of actors waiting for him, such as there had never been before in England.

The Elizabethan theatre

The Elizabethan stage

The Elizabethan theatres were not like the ones we know today. Their form derived from the inn yards and animal-baiting rings in which actors had been accustomed to perform in the past. They were circular wooden buildings, with a paved courtyard in the middle open to the sky. A rectangular stage jutted out from the side of the building into the middle of this yard. Some of the audience stood in the yard (or 'pit') to watch the play. They were thus on three sides of the stage, and much closer to it than an audience sitting in a modern theatre. These 'groundlings' paid only a penny to get in, but for wealthier spectators there were seats in three covered tiers or balconies in the sides of the building overlooking the pit and the stage. Shakespeare aptly called such a theatre a 'wooden O' in the Prologue to *Henry V* (line 13).

The stage itself was partially covered by a roof which projected from the wall at the rear of the stage and was supported by two posts in front. On either side at the back of the stage was a door. These led to the dressing room (or 'tiring house') and it was by means of these doors that actors entered and left the stage. It would have been on one of these doors, locked by Aumerle, that both York and the Duchess of York knocked in *Richard II*, V.3.37 and 73. Between the doors was a small recess or alcove which was curtained off. This might, indeed, be simply another, middle, doorway into the tiring house. Such a 'discovery place', as it was called, was too small to allow any action to take place within it.

Above the discovery place was a balcony. This might be used as a privileged place for some noblemen or high-paying spectators to sit (such people might, indeed, actually sit on seats around the edge of the stage), but it was also used, for example, for scenes such as the balcony scenes in *Romeo and Juliet* (II.2 and III.5). The balcony would have been used in performances of *Richard II*. In I.1 Richard would have been seated there with his nobles, while Henry and Mowbray argued on the main stage below (at I.1.186 Richard asks Henry to 'throw up' to him the gage he is holding). In I.3 Richard would again have been on the balcony, for at I.3.54 he 'descends' to embrace Henry, which he could have done by using the stairs which led down to the tiring house and then going through one of the doors on to the stage. Most effectively of all, in III.3.61 when Henry and his followers see Richard come out on the battlements of Flint Castle, it would have been on the balcony that he appeared. And when, at line 171, Richard comes down to meet Henry with the words 'Down, down I come like glistering Phaethon', that he did actually descend would have stressed the symbolism of the moment. Richard is coming down from his high place as king.

Such 'public theatres', as they are called to distinguish them from the smaller, indoor 'private' theatres built early in the seventeenth century, could hold about three thousand spectators. The yards were about 70ft in diameter and the rectangular stages approximately 40ft by 30ft and 5ft 6in high. Shakespeare's company performed at James Burbage's Theatre until 1596, and used the Swan and the Curtain until they moved into their own new theatre, the Globe, in 1599.

Elizabethan performances

Performances in the public theatres were continuous and there was very little scenery. Scene divisions were only added to most of Shakespeare's plays much later by eighteenth-century editors. The early quarto editions of *Richard II* have neither act nor scene divisions. These divisions are still retained in modern editions of the plays because they make reference easier, but they should not mislead the student into supposing there was any real break in the play such as there is in the theatre today when the curtains are closed and the set is changed. That is why, in our play, Gaunt leaves at I.1.195, before the end of the scene, in order to be ready to begin I.2, which would follow immediately. 'Continuous staging' means that an Elizabethan performance would have been shorter than a modern one: in the Prologue to *Romeo and Juliet* the Chorus speaks of 'two hours' as the acting time (line 12; compare *Henry VIII*, Prologue, line 13).

Not only were performances quicker; they were also more fluid. We are used to each scene being set clearly in one place, represented by the set on the stage, which is changed when the location of the action changes with a new scene. This was not the case in an Elizabethan theatre. The setting might change actually in the course of the scene.

THE GLOBE PLAYHOUSE

The theatre, originally built by James Burbage in 1576, was made of wood (Burbage had been trained as a carpenter). It was situated to the north of the River Thames on Shoreditch in Finsbury Fields. There was trouble with the lease of the land, and so the theatre was dismantled in 1598, and reconstructed 'in an other forme' on the south side of the Thames as the Globe. Its sign is thought to have been a figure of the Greek hero Hercules carrying the globe. It was built in six months, its galleries being roofed with thatch. This caught fire in 1613 when some smouldering wadding, from a cannon used in a performance of Shakespeare's *Henry VIII*, lodged in it. The theatre was burnt down, and when it was rebuilt again on the old foundations, the galleries were roofed with tiles.

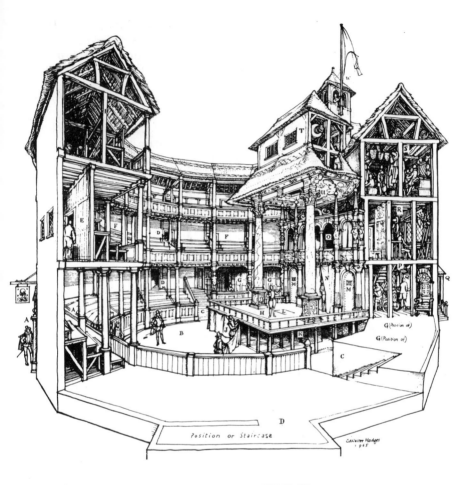

A CONJECTURAL RECONSTRUCTION OF THE INTERIOR OF
THE GLOBE PLAYHOUSE

AA Main entrance
 B The Yard
CC Entrances to lowest gallery
 D Entrance to staircase and upper galleries
 E Corridor serving the different sections of the
   middle gallery
 F Middle gallery ('Twopenny Rooms')
 G 'Gentlemen's Rooms or Lords Rooms'
 H The stage
 J The hanging being put up round the stage
 K The 'Hell' under the stage
 L The stage trap, leading down to the Hell
MM Stage doors

 N Curtained 'place behind the stage'
 O Gallery above the stage, used as required
   sometimes by musicians, sometimes by
   spectators, and often as part of the play
 P Back-stage area (the tiring-house)
 Q Tiring-house door
 R Dressing-rooms
 S Wardrobe and storage
 T The hut housing the machine for lowering
   enthroned gods, etc., to the stage
 U The 'Heavens'
 W Hoisting the playhouse flag

During the first part of III.3, Richard is on the castle battlements (that is, on the stage balcony) while Henry and his followers are supposed to be outside the castle walls (that is, on the main stage). However, when Richard comes down to meet Henry in a courtyard of the castle (lines 178–82), he actually enters the main stage and meets him there, so now the stage represents the interior of the castle. Hence, in this scene the stage has represented two places (outside and inside the castle) but the acting goes on regardless.

It is because of the continuous staging and the lack of scenery that characters in Shakespeare's plays often tell the audience what locality is to be imagined at different moments. At the end of I.1, Richard tells us that the trial by combat which we shall see in I.3 is to be held at Coventry, and Gaunt reminds us of this in I.2 (I.1.198–9, I.2.56). At I.4.58 Bushy informs Richard that the dying Gaunt is at Ely House, so that when, in a moment, we meet Gaunt in the next scene, we know where we are. When Richard returns from Ireland his first words tell us where he is (III.2.1). At the end of II.3 we learn Henry will go to Bristol Castle, which is where III.1 is set (II.3.163) and at the end of III.2 Richard tells us he will retreat to Flint Castle, where III.3 occurs (III.2.209).

However, Shakespeare is by no means always concerned to reassure us like this. Dramatic effectiveness is always the criterion: Shakespeare feels no need to be realistic and accurate for its own sake. So there is often no evidence at all in the text for where a scene is set. Modern editors often supply a locale for such scenes, setting I.1, for example, at Windsor Castle, which is where this event occurred historically, though Shakespeare does not mention the fact. But we can be confident that if Shakespeare's characters do not tell us where they are it does not matter.

The lack of a curtain across the stage in the Elizabethan theatre explains why scenes often end with rhyming lines. These show the audience that the scene *has* ended, and prepare them for a new scene (for example, the final lines of III.3, III.4, IV.1, and V.5 of *Richard II*). And because actors were in full view from the moment they set foot on the stage, entrances and exits had to be written in as part of the play. Actors could not come on to the stage and get ready for a scene; it would seem very odd for them only to begin speaking once everyone was in position. That is why characters often say that they are coming or going, to cover these movements (for example, in our play, I.2.74, I.4.63–5, II.1.221–2). Alternatively, a scene may begin in mid-conversation, with the characters talking as they enter the stage (for example, I.4.1, II.1.1, III.3.1), or another character may announce their entrance to fill the time they take to reach their positions (as in II.1.69). For the same reason, dead bodies had always to be removed by the actors in the course of the play (so Richard's body is carried off at V.5.117 and V.6.51–2 and Gaunt leaves the stage to die at II.1.138).

Shakespeare's dramatic career

For such theatres Shakespeare wrote, between about 1588 and 1613, thirty-seven plays, as well as contributing to some by other dramatists. The order in which these plays were written, and their dates, are matters of doubt. Some of his plays were published before Shakespeare's death, but in these cases, although of course the plays must have been written before they were published, we do not know how long before. Sometimes there are references to contemporary events in the plays themselves which help us to date them. The difficulty, though, is in recognising such references. We can be more confident when we know when a play was first performed. It must have been written shortly before this. Unfortunately, the first performances of many of his plays are not recorded. Often, scholars can only argue for a date on the basis of their understanding of the development of Shakespeare's art.

Shakespeare's development

Despite these difficulties over the dating of individual plays, the broad lines of Shakespeare's dramatic career are now plain. He began in the late 1580s and early 1590s with comedies which depended for their effect upon funny situation and surprises, like *The Comedy of Errors* (1590–3) and plays dealing with English history, like the three plays of *Henry VI* (1589–91). This was the period of his apprenticeship. During the 1590s he developed his mastery of these kinds of play to write comic masterpieces such as *As You Like It* (1599–1600) and *Twelfth Night* (1599–1600) and history plays such as the two plays of *Henry IV* (1597–8) and *Henry V* (1598–9).

As the century ends, however, a new and more sombre note enters his work, which leads, in the early 1600s, to the period of Shakespeare's great tragedies — *Hamlet* (1600–1), *Othello* (1602–3), *King Lear* (1605–6) and *Macbeth* (1605–6). Because of the very different mood of these plays this first decade of the seventeenth century is sometimes distinguished from the earlier 'Elizabethan' period as the 'Jacobean' phase of Shakespeare's career.

And then, finally, in the last years of his dramatic career, Shakespeare wrote a small group of plays of an entirely new kind. The 'romances', *Pericles* (1608–9), *Cymbeline* (1609–10) *The Winter's Tale* (1610–11) and *The Tempest* (1611–12), all have happy endings, but they are not at all like the comedies of the first period. In all of these plays the characters have known or experience great sadness. Shakespeare does not, as in the early comedies, ignore sorrow and suffering, but neither does it threaten to overwhelm him as in the great tragedies. These very beautiful plays all end on a note of hope for the future. Their great theme is reconciliation.

The place of *Richard II* in Shakespeare's career

Richard II was first published in 1597, and scholars now believe it was written and first performed in 1595. For the Elizabethans Richard's reign and deposition were crucial, for to them they owed, ultimately, the presence on the throne of their own Queen Elizabeth I. And for Shakespeare personally, at that point in his career, to turn to Richard's reign for the subject of a play was to make possible a larger dramatic design incorporating many plays.

The Elizabethan view of Richard II

In the mind of the Elizabethans the deposition of Richard II began a series of events which led to the Tudor dynasty and the reign of Elizabeth I. In 1548 Edward Hall published a prose chronicle history which was to be one of the sources of Shakespeare's play. Its full title was:

> The Union of the Two Noble and Illustrious Families of Lancaster and York, being long in continual dissension for the crown of this noble realm, with all the acts done in both the times of the Princes, both of the one lineage and of the other, beginning at the time of king Henry the fourth, the first author of this division, and so successively proceeding to the reign of the high and prudent prince king Henry the eighth, the indubitable flower and very heir of both the said lineages.

This long title tells us three things about the sixteenth-century attitude to earlier English history:

(*i*)   Hall sees fifteenth-century English history, from the accession of Henry IV in 1399 to the defeat and death of Richard III at the battle of Bosworth Field in 1485, as a self-contained period which tells a single story.

(*ii*) This story has a clear beginning in the deposition of Richard II by Henry Bolingbroke. Richard was the last English king to rule by clear hereditary right, descended in direct succession from William the Conqueror (1066–87), and to Hall, as to the Elizabethans generally, the deposition of this rightful monarch was disastrous. Once the crown was taken by a usurper, it became the object of rivalry amongst powerful princes and noblemen who each wanted it for himself. The result was a series of bloody wars (the Wars of the Roses) between two main factions: the House of Lancaster (the descendants of John of Gaunt, whose badge was a red rose) and the House of York (the descendants of Edmund of Langley, whose badge was a white rose).

(*iii*) This story of civil war has for Hall a clear ending. Henry Tudor
defeated the last Yorkist king, Richard III, to become Henry VII.
He claimed descent from John of Gaunt, Duke of Lancaster and so,
when he married the Yorkist heiress, Richard III's niece Elizabeth,
the two warring families were at last united. Their son, Henry VIII
hence had no rival: and his daughter was Elizabeth I.

So, for Shakespeare and his fellow Elizabethans, the deposition of
Richard II was the beginning of the historical story which ended with
their own queen. It was, for them, the original cause of the stable and
ordered society in which they lived, not something irrelevant, shut away
in the past.

Richard II and Shakespeare's other history plays

Shakespeare wrote in all ten history plays. Of these one, *Henry VIII*, was
written at the end of his career (1612–13), long after the other history
plays, and one, *King John* (1597) dealt with an isolated period of early
medieval English history to which Shakespeare did not return. However,
the remaining eight belong together. They tell the entire story of English
history from the fall of Richard II in 1399 to the death of Richard III in
1485—that is, the story of Hall's chronicle. These eight plays thus form a
cycle which covers nearly a century of English history, and it is that
century which, as we have seen, was so crucial to the Elizabethans.

However, Shakespeare did not write these eight plays in order.
Scholars have established that they were written in two groups, of four
plays each, and that the first group dealt with the later period of history.
The two groups (or tetralogies) are:

(*i*) FIRST TETRALOGY: written 1590–3, this consists of the three parts
of *Henry VI* and *Richard III*, which cover the years 1422–85.
(*ii*) SECOND TETRALOGY: written 1595–1598/9, this consists of
Richard II, the two parts of *Henry IV* and *Henry V*, which cover the
years 1399–1422.

Thus, when Shakespeare turned to *Richard II* in 1595 he had written the
first tetralogy; that is to say, he had written the *end* of the story and was
now turning to its beginning. And he followed *Richard II* with the two
parts of *Henry IV* and *Henry V* in order. This suggests that when he
began *Richard II* he may have already formulated the idea of a complete
cycle of plays and that he deliberately wrote *Richard II* not only as a
complete play in its own right, but as a prologue to the full cycle of plays
which he then went on to complete. We notice, for example, the many
prophecies of the suffering and bloodshed that England will endure
because of Richard's failings as king and his deposition by Henry (for

example, II.1.200–8, II.2.9–13, III.3.93–100, IV.1.134–49, V.1.55–68). That so many people foretell civil war stresses the fact that what we see in *Richard II* will have dire consequences in the future that lies beyond the play—that is, in the years which are treated in the other history plays. This is underlined by the end of the play, which does not have any satisfying neatness, any sense of completion, about it. Henry has already suffered the Abbot of Westminster's rebellion, he is worried about his son's fitness to inherit the throne, and he feels guilt and remorse for Richard's death. There is no sense of triumph, of something finally achieved, in Henry's final speech. Clearly, though the action of *Richard II* ends Richard's story, it only begins a larger story, and our attention is called to this fact.

The publication of the plays

Quartos

Nineteen of Shakespeare's plays were printed during his lifetime in what are called 'quartos' from the fact that these books, which each contained one play, were made up of sheets of paper each folded twice to make *four* leaves. Shakespeare, however, did not supervise the publication of these plays. This was not unusual; when a playwright sold a play to a dramatic company he sold all his rights in it. There was then no copyright protection for an author, so a writer had no control over what happened to his work. Anyone who could get hold of the text of a play from a playhouse might print it if he wanted to. Actors (or even members of the audience) might publish what they could remember of the text of a play. Clearly, texts produced like this would be unreliable.

The First Folio

In 1623 John Heming and Henry Condell, two actors in Shakespeare's company, collected together thirty-six of Shakespeare's plays (*Pericles* was omitted) and published them in a large folio (so called since in such a book the sheets of paper are folded once to give *two* leaves). This, the First Folio, was followed by later editions in 1632, 1663 and 1685. Shakespeare, of course, had not been alive to check the text of the First Folio. Furthermore, the plays as printed in the Folio often differ from the earlier quartos, leaving a modern editor with the problem of deciding which version is nearest to Shakespeare's original playscript. In addition there are many printed errors. It is because editors correct these errors in different ways, and sometimes prefer the quarto text, sometimes the Folio text, that different modern editions of Shakespeare's plays vary.

Shakespeare's use of sources

Shakespeare based *R.chard II* (and all his history plays) on the historical sources available to him, but he did not follow them with anything like a scholar's precision and care. He took from his sources only those facts which would serve his play, and was quite ready to omit details or change the order of events. He did not feel any obligation to be faithful to facts as facts. Whether his Richard was actually like the historical Richard was not a question which concerned him. He was making a play about a particular kind of man and king: *that* was what concerned him. As a result, his play may not be a very reliable guide to fourteenth-century English history, but it is a fine exploration of the characters and predicaments of men in all ages.

The sources which scholars have discovered for *Richard II* are the following:

(1) Edward Hall, *The Union of the Two Noble ... Families of Lancaster and York* (1548). This chronicle history deals with the history of England from the end of Richard II's reign, through the Wars of the Roses, to Henry VII and the founding of the Tudor dynasty. It seems to have supplied the material for V.2-3, and may have suggested to Shakespeare the plan for his complete cycle of history plays (see pp. 14–15).

(2) Raphael Holinshed, *Chronicles of England, Scotland and Ireland* (1586–7). Holinshed's account of Richard II's reign supplied the general outline of events and historical facts for Shakespeare's play.

(3) Jean Froissart, *Chroniques*, translated into English by John Bourchier, Lord Berners (1523–5). Froissart was a Frenchman who visited Edward III's court in the 1360s and actually lived at Richard II's court. He is, in his *Chronicles*, very sympathetic to Richard, and may have suggested to Shakespeare the noble character of Gaunt (who in Holinshed is an ignoble self-seeker) and the idea for Gaunt's last speeches and rebukes to Richard in II.1.

(4) Samuel Daniel, *The Civil Wars between Lancaster and York* (1595). This long poem by a contemporary English poet of Shakespeare's probably supplied the clue for the love between Richard and his queen (Daniel, like Shakespeare, makes her older than she actually was) and suggested the scene of their parting, V.1.

(5) *Thomas of Woodstock* (not published until 1870). An anonymous play which, centred on the Duke of Gloucester and his murder, deals with Richard II's reign between 1382 and 1397, that is, with the events immediately preceding those in Shakespeare's play. It may have suggested the favourable view of Gloucester we find in *Richard II* (II.1.128) and the character of the Duchess of Gloucester (I.2). Perhaps

Shakespeare took the idea of presenting Gaunt as a wise and patriotic counsellor from the similar presentation of Gloucester in *Woodstock*. But, as the play was not printed in Elizabethan times, we cannot be sure that it was actually written before *Richard II*.

(6) George Ferrers, William Baldwin and others, *The Mirror for Magistrates* (1559). A massive collection of verse tales about the tragic fall of princes and nobles, the *Mirror* includes the stories of the Duke of Gloucester, Thomas Mowbray, the Earl of Northumberland and Richard II himself, and may have given Shakespeare hints for a number of details.

Additional sources (including medieval French chronicles and a lost play on Richard II) have been suggested by some scholars, but whether Shakespeare read them is a matter of doubt. The way Shakespeare handled his source material is a more interesting question, for it sheds light on his aims in writing the play. The alterations he made are of the following kinds.

(1) *The omission of unsuitable material:* Richard's campaign in Ireland, of which we hear nothing (not even whether it was a success or not) is a notable example of this. By such omissions Shakespeare gives a clear and simple line to the action of the play. It concentrates on Richard's decline and Henry's rise without any digressions.

(2) *The alteration of events:* A conspicuous example is that in Holinshed Northumberland takes Richard to Flint Castle as a prisoner while in *Richard II* Henry and Northumberland find Richard there unexpectedly. This change makes Henry appear less cunning and active, more the favourite of fortune, than in Holinshed (see scene summary of III.3).

(3) *The addition of events:* Examples of additions to the source material are Gaunt's famous speech in II.1.31–68, the behaviour of the Duchess of York in V.2–3, and (most significantly) the three scenes centred on the queen (II.2.1–72, III.4, V.1). Only for the last of these was there a clue in Daniel (for their purpose, see the scene summaries).

(4) *The addition of symbolic actions and images:* By introducing these, Shakespeare stresses and clarifies the themes of the play: examples include the recurrent sun imagery (see p. 97), the Crown (mentioned throughout the play, notably in III.2.160–77 and used by Richard as a stage property in IV.1.180–8), mirrors and shadows (again notably in IV.1.263–301).

(5) *The isolation of the figure of Richard:* Shakespeare centres his play more firmly than any source on the figure of Richard himself, devoting much attention (especially after the return from Ireland in III.2) to the

confusions and despair of Richard's mind and the pathos and tragedy of his situation.

(6) *The alteration of the order of events:* The scene summary of IV.1 shows a conspicuous example of this.

(7) *The telescoping of events:* For dramatic effect Shakespeare runs together events actually separated in time. A good example is II.1, where events covering six months appear to follow one another directly (see the scene summary).

(8) *The alteration of characters' ages and relationships:* The Queen (actually only eleven years old in 1399) appears as a mature woman and the Duchess of York, actually Aumerle's stepmother, acts and speaks like his mother (V.2.103–11). The former change allows the achievement of pathos in the Queen's sorrow for Richard, the latter the Duchess's real anxiety about Aumerle's fate.

(9) *The introduction of details in anticipation of the later Henry IV plays:* The mention of Prince Hal (V.3.1–12) and the youth of Harry Percy (II.3.36–44) are examples of details which serve little purpose in *Richard II* but which do anticipate the situation Shakespeare was to handle in *1* and *2 Henry IV* (see the notes on these lines).

A note on the text

Richard II was first published in a quarto in 1597. This text (Q1) is usually free from error, and may have been printed from Shakespeare's own manuscript. It therefore forms the basis of any modern edition of the play as it is the copy nearest to Shakespeare's original. Q1 was reprinted twice the following year, 1598 (Q2 and Q3), but each time the printer set up his type he added errors to the text.

None of these quartos includes the deposition scene (IV.1.154–319). The censor probably thought that, at a time of uncertainty about the succession to the throne (Elizabeth, now an old woman, was unmarried and childless), it was unwise to allow the public to read about the dethroning of an earlier childless monarch, especially since Elizabeth was likened to Richard by her critics. Those who disapproved of the Queen's reign accused her, as Richard had been accused, of having favourites, of neglecting the kingdom, of being a tyrant and of wasting money. And they pointed to Richard's fate as a warning of what might become of her. That *Richard II* was politically dangerous we have clear evidence. When Robert Devereux, Earl of Essex, planned to overthrow Queen Elizabeth, his supporters arranged for *Richard II* to be performed at the Globe on the eve of the rebellion in February 1601. They undoubtedly felt that the play justified Henry's usurpation of Richard's throne and wanted the performance of this to win popular support in London for their intended dethroning of Elizabeth. In fact, the play refuses to take sides as clearly as this, and in the deposition scene a good deal of sympathy is excited for Richard (see p. 65). This may explain why, when the rebellion failed, no action was taken against Shakespeare or his company, the Chamberlain's Men.

Elizabeth died in 1603 and James I had succeeded her peacefully five years before Q4 was published in 1608. Hence, the security of the monarchy was no longer a delicate matter, and this quarto was able to advertise on its title-page 'new additions' to the play, namely, the previously unprinted deposition scene. Where the printer of Q4 got his copy for this scene is not known, but, whatever it was, his source was not very reliable. The deposition scene as it appears in Q4, and the reprint of 1615 (Q5), is full of errors.

The Folio text of 1623 (F1) is based on Q3, and Q5 for some passages at the end of the play. It would not, therefore, be very useful in the ordinary way, since it takes us still further from Q1. However, F1 adds many stage directions not found in the earlier quartos (these are printed in the Penguin edition of the play) and often corrects their texts. It seems probable that these improvements were made by comparing the quartos with the theatre prompt-book (that is, the manuscript copy of the play actually used by the actors) and correcting the printed text where it did not agree with the prompt-book. Furthermore, F1 has a much better text of the deposition scene than Q4 (probably from the same prompt-book). Hence, a modern editor will follow F1 for that scene, and will incorporate into his text based on Q1, such of the corrections in F1 as he believes are improvements which reflect what Shakespeare actually wrote.

All references to *Richard II* in these Notes are to Stanley Wells's New Penguin Shakespeare edition of the play, Penguin Books, Harmondsworth, 1969. Act and scene divisions are the same in all modern editions of the play, but line numbers may vary from edition to edition. This variation should not, however, be so great as to prevent anyone using a different edition from finding a reference in his text.

All references to Shakespeare's other plays are to the texts printed in William Shakespeare, *The Complete Works*, edited by Peter Alexander, Collins, London, 1951, but again, it should be easy to locate these references in any good edition of Shakespeare.

Part 2

Summaries
of RICHARD II

A general summary

Act I: Richard as king (April 1398–February 1399)

In the spring of 1398 Richard II, King of England, has come to hear an accusation of treason laid by his cousin, Henry Bolingbroke, Duke of Hereford, against Thomas Mowbray, Duke of Norfolk. Henry charges Mowbray with misusing money given him by the King to pay his soldiers, of being responsible for all the plots against Richard during the last eighteen years, and, in particular, with being responsible for the murder of Richard's and Henry's uncle, Thomas of Woodstock, Duke of Gloucester. Mowbray denies the charges and Richard, unable to reconcile the two men, appoints St Lambert's Day (17 September) for them to settle the issue by single combat. Before that occurs in I.3, we learn in I.2 from John of Gaunt, Duke of Lancaster, Henry's father and a brother of Gloucester, that Richard himself was implicated in Gloucester's death. Gaunt refuses the pleas of the Duchess of Gloucester to avenge Gloucester himself, saying that no subject may punish God's deputy on earth, the King. In I.3, just as the trial by combat is about to begin, Richard unexpectedly stops it and banishes both men, Mowbray for life, Henry for ten years, which he reduces to six when he sees Gaunt's sorrow. In the following scene, I.4, we see Richard for the first time not on a formal state occasion, and he appears a very unpleasant person, jealous of Henry's popular support, resolved to finance his expedition against Irish rebels by illegal and tyrannical means, and callous when he hears that Gaunt is dying.

Act II: the beginning of Richard's decline (February 1399–July 1399)

The act begins with Gaunt foretelling that Richard's extravagant and irresponsible way of life cannot last long. Gaunt is deeply distressed at the way the England he loves is neglected and mistreated by the King. When Richard enters, Gaunt rebukes him, but this only makes Richard angry. A moment after Gaunt has left the stage we hear that he has died and Richard immediately plans to seize his wealth (rightfully now the inheritance of Gaunt's son, Henry) to finance the Irish campaign.

Gaunt's brother, Edmund of Langley, Duke of York, protests at this, and foretells dire consequences if Richard denies Henry his rights, but Richard is not dissuaded. As the scene ends, we hear that already Henry has an invasion force prepared to sail for England as soon as Richard leaves for Ireland. In the next scene, II.2, the anxiety of the Queen, Isabel, increases our sense of foreboding, just before we learn from York that Henry has landed and that he, as Governor of England in Richard's absence, is ill-prepared to resist him. The scene ends with Richard's favourites, Bushy, Bagot and Green, resolving to flee for fear of the revenge of the people against them. In II.3, Henry and Northumberland proceed through England, gathering support, until they come to Berkeley Castle, where York tries to persuade Henry to lay down his arms. Henry protests that he has come not to harm Richard but to gain his rights as Duke of Lancaster, and York admits he can do nothing to stop him. In II.4 the Welsh army which had been gathered to fight for Richard tires of waiting for him to return from Ireland and disbands.

Act III: the submission of Richard (July 1399–August 1399)

Henry, at Bristol Castle, executes Bushy and Green, who had taken refuge there (III.1). In III.2 Richard finally returns from Ireland and has high hopes his mere presence will win support, but a succession of ill-tidings (the disbanding of the Welsh army, the extent of popular and noble support for Henry, the execution of his favourites and the desertion of York to Henry) plunge him into despair and he discharges his followers. From now on our sympathy is won increasingly to Richard. At Flint Castle in III.3 he immediately grants Henry's demand for his rights as Duke of Lancaster, although he is convinced that Henry is really after the crown. He leaves for London, in Henry's power. The act ends with the 'garden scene' (III.4) in which the Queen hears of Henry's success from a gardener and decides to go herself to London.

Act IV: the deposition of Richard (September 1399–December 1399)

At the beginning of the act nobles argue fiercely about who was, or was not, responsible for Gloucester's death. Henry has just ordered that the various charges shall be settled by combat when York enters to say that Richard will willingly give up his crown. He hails Henry as King Henry IV. At this the Bishop of Carlisle protests, and, in a strong speech, argues that no subject can judge a king, let alone force him to abdicate. For this he is charged with treason. Richard enters, and does give Henry the crown, but he cannot bring himself to make a public declaration of his faults. He is deeply disturbed in his mind and, although Henry has arranged the whole affair and has his way, it is Richard who is at the centre of the scene and who wins our sympathy as he shames the nobles present as his betrayers. The act ends with the Abbot of Westminster, the Bishop of Carlisle, and the Duke of Aumerle, York's son, discussing a plot to overthrow Henry and restore Richard.

Act V: rebellion and the death of Richard
(December 1399–March 1400)

In V.1 the Queen meets Richard on his way to the Tower. Their conversation is interrupted by Northumberland, who says Richard must now go to Pomfret Castle in Yorkshire, and the Queen to France. They take a final farewell. In V.2 York discovers from Aumerle the plot against Henry and, as he has sworn loyalty to Henry and guaranteed Aumerle's loyalty to the new king, he is determined, despite the pleas of the Duchess of York, to go immediately to reveal the treason to Henry. The Duchess sends Aumerle to reach Henry before York, and intends to follow as quickly as she can. At the beginning of V.3 we find Henry troubled by the reckless behaviour of his son who, it seems, will not make a very suitable heir to the throne. Aumerle then bursts in and, in private, asks, and receives, Henry's pardon before Henry knows what it is he was going to do. But when York arrives, the plot is revealed, and York insists Aumerle should not be pardoned. He is interrupted by the Duchess knocking on the door, and she, just as vehemently, begs that Aumerle should be pardoned. Henry, not quite sure whether to take all this clamour and contradiction seriously, does pardon Aumerle, but arranges for the other rebels to be pursued. In V.4 Sir Piers of Exton determines to kill Richard so, thereby, he believes, relieving Henry of a great worry. Alone in his prison, in V.5, Richard meditates on his sorrow. When the murderers come, he puts up a brave fight, but it is in vain. In the last scene of the play we hear that the rebellion has been crushed. When Sir Piers brings Richard's body to Henry, he receives no thanks. On the contrary, Henry is filled with shame and guilt, and the play ends with him planning a crusade 'To wash this blood from off my guilty hand'.

Detailed summaries

Act I Scene 1

Richard is himself to be at the centre of this play and the drama begins by presenting him to us in his full royal majesty. Theatrically, the presentation of a full court in the first scene makes a spectacular opening to the play. The most important function of the monarch is that he is the source of justice (prosecutions of criminals in modern English law courts are still made in the name of the Queen) and we here meet Richard in that capacity. He has come to hear a charge of treason made by his cousin, Henry Bolingbroke, Duke of Hereford, against Thomas Mowbray, Duke of Norfolk. (This 'appeal', or accusation, was made on 29 April 1398, at Windsor, but Shakespeare mentions neither the time nor the place.) Bolingbroke speaks vigorously, but it is some time before he makes specific charges. When he does they are three in number: (*i*) that Mowbray has misused for his own advantage money given him by the King; (*ii*) that he has been responsible for all the plots during the past eighteen years; and (*iii*) that he was guilty of murdering Richard's and Henry's uncle, Thomas of Woodstock, Duke of Gloucester. These charges Mowbray denies, and in return himself accuses Henry of treason. Richard endeavours to reconcile the two noblemen, but in vain, and so he appoints a day for them to settle the matter by trial by combat.

Throughout this scene Richard conducts himself as befits a king: he speaks royally, claims to be impartial and seems anxious to restore peace and goodwill. Yet already there are signs that he is not quite the just king he seems. As Shakespeare's audience probably knew (and would, in any case, learn in the next scene) Richard had himself ordered Mowbray to kill Gloucester. If, then, Henry knows of Mowbray's guilt, he may well know of Richard's. That he does know is perhaps suggested by his reference to the murder of Abel (line 104): Abel was slain by his close kinsman Cain, as Gloucester was by his kinsman Richard. That Richard fears his own guilt may be disclosed is suggested in line 109, where he sees Henry's accusation as an attack on himself. That Richard should deny that Henry is his heir (line 116), even ironically, shows that the idea that Henry is after the crown has crossed his mind. Thus, behind the formal surface of the occasion there is a bitter family quarrel: it is Henry, Edward III's grandson, like Richard, who is *really* the champion of justice, and not Richard, the King. The frequent references here to murder and blood further create an atmosphere of suspense and foreboding.

NOTES AND GLOSSARY:

King Richard:	Richard of Bordeaux was born in 1367, only son of Edward, the Black Prince, eldest son and heir of Edward III; the Black Prince died in 1376 and Richard succeeded Edward III in 1377—he has thus ruled for twenty-one years when the play opens, but is only thirty-one years old
John of Gaunt:	John of Ghent (his birthplace is Flanders), Duke of Lancaster, was the fourth son of Edward III, and so Richard's uncle; born in 1340, he is fifty-eight years old when the play opens

Lord Marshal:	the Duke of Surrey (who appears in IV.1) acted on behalf of Mowbray, the Earl Marshal (in charge of heraldry and state occasions) on this occasion, but whether Shakespeare identified the two characters is not clear (see notes on pages 37 and 66)
band:	bond
Henry Hereford:	Henry of Bolingbroke (his birthplace in Lincoln-shire), Duke of Hereford (in Elizabethan pronun-ciation, only two syllables, 'Herford') was borne in 1367 by John of Gaunt's first wife, Blanche of Lan-caster; he is thus Richard's exact contempor-ary and his cousin
late appeal:	recent accusation of treason; Henry accused Mowbray of treason at a parliament at Shrewsbury in January 1398 and both men were ordered to appear later before the King to settle the matter
our:	it was a convention for kings to use the plural forms of pronouns
our ... hear:	that is, our want of leisure would not let us hear
Thomas Mowbray:	Thomas Mowbray, Duke of Norfolk, was born about 1366 and died in Venice in 1399
sounded:	asked
If ... malice:	whether he accuses Mowbray because of some old grudge
sift him:	discover his true feelings
argument:	subject
On ... malice:	it is because he has detected some clear threat posed to your highness by Mowbray, and not because of any confirmed hatred he bears him
And ... hear:	that is, showing favour to neither
High-stomached:	proud, stubborn
Bolingbroke:	pronounced (and spelled) 'Bullingbrook' in Shake-speare's time
Each...happiness:	may each day so improve on the happiness of previous days
hap:	fortune
Add ... crown:	that is, until you receive immortal happiness in heaven
cause ... come:	cause about which you come
thou:	the informal language of affection, used between members of a family, changed to the formal 'you' when Richard is trying to assert his authority (line 186); modern English has lost this distinction then possible in the singular ('you' in line 25 is plural)

heaven...record:	may heaven be the witness; Henry begins by clearing himself of the suspicion of personal malice Richard had expressed at lines 8–10
Tendering:	valuing, cherishing
from other:	from all other motives
appellant:	accuser
My ... earth:	that is, I will prove by mortal combat
divine:	immortal
miscreant:	literally 'unbeliever', but used as a general term of contempt
good:	high in rank (the idea is developed in lines 41–2)
aggravate the note:	increase the reproach, stress the disgrace
right-drawn:	drawn from the sheath in a just cause
Let...zeal:	may my moderate language not call in doubt the fervour of my loyalty
woman's war:	that is, fighting with words, verbal argument
eager:	sharp
arbitrate:	decide
hot, cooled:	both heated in anger and warm since Henry is alive; it must be 'cooled' in death by Mowbray's sword
naught...say:	say nothing at all
reverence of:	respect for
reins and spurs:	to hold the reins loosely and apply spurs to a horse would make him gallop; Mowbray means that Richard's royal presence prevents him from replying in passionate anger
post:	ride swiftly (post horses were kept at inns on main roads to allow messengers to travel quickly by changing horses at frequent intervals)
high ... royalty:	that is, his kinship to Richard
let him be:	assuming that he is (in the ordinary way it would be dangerous to accuse a member of the King's family of treason)
maintain:	prove
odds:	advantage
And meet him:	and still meet him
tied:	bound, obliged
Alps:	mountains of south central Europe
inhabitable:	uninhabitable
this:	that is, his sword
hopes:	that is, hopes of Heaven
gage:	pledge; by throwing down an object (usually a glove) the challenger pledged himself to fight whoever took it up

Disclaiming ... King: taking up Mowbray's words at lines 58–9 Henry rejects the protection of his royal blood
except: take exception to, use as an excuse
honour's pawn: the pledge of his honour referred to at line 69
gently: nobly
Which ... shoulder: men were made knights by being touched on each shoulder ('dubbed') with a sword held by a knight; Mowbray was probably knighted by Richard, which would make the reference a polite compliment which seems to have secured Richard's goodwill in Richard's next words, lines 84–6
answer: that is, answer your charges by meeting you in combat
in ... trial: in any proper manner or chivalric form of knightly combat
inherit us: possess us with, make us think
Look what: whatever
noble: gold coin worth about 33p
lendings: pay
lewd employments: improper use
Fetch: derive
first ... spring: originator
Duke ... death: Thomas of Woodstock (his birthplace), Duke of Gloucester, was born in 1355, the seventh and youngest son of Edward III; he was thus the brother of Gaunt and York and the uncle of Richard and Henry: an opponent of Richard's policies, he was charged with treason and killed at Calais in 1397, almost certainly by Mowbray on Richard's orders; this was certainly the view of Shakespeare's time, found in Holinshed, and put by Gaunt in the next scene (I.2.37–41); this third charge by Henry is, of course, the crucial one, and (as Richard's reply, line 109, shows) the one that comes near the King
Suggest ... adversaries: persuaded his (Gloucester's) enemies, who were only too ready to believe it, that he was guilty of treason
consequently subsequently
Sluiced: let out
Abel: in the biblical story the innocent Abel was slain by his brother Cain who was jealous of Abel's favour with God, and Abel's blood cried out from the ground for vengeance (Genesis 4:1–16): the reference can be seen as a sly attack on Richard—as

Abel was slain by his kinsman Cain, so Gloucester was slain by his kinsman Richard; it stresses Gloucester's innocence (by likening him to Abel) and Mowbray's wickedness (as the first murderer, Cain is a particularly horrible figure), and it underlines the fact that, despite the formality of the occasion, this is a *family* quarrel

tongueless: silent, dumb

rough chastisement: harsh punishment

glorious ... descent: nobility of my family line

pitch: the highest point of a falcon's flight: this is a crucial line, for in seeing that Henry aims high, Richard in this aside recognises that Henry's previous speech had been directed at him, the highest in the land; it may be that Richard already suspects Henry of ambitious designs on the crown; whether or not Henry *does* yet have them we do not know

this ... blood: this disgrace (Henry) to his (Richard's) blood

sceptre: staff carried by a monarch as a symbol of royal authority

awe: reverence due to

Should nothing: shall not in any way

partialize: make partial, make me favour him

receipt: money received

duly: properly

For that: because of

remainder ... account: payment outstanding on a large debt

fetch ... queen: Mowbray went to France in 1395 to arrange Richard's marriage to Isabel, and he means that Richard had not paid him back his expenses for this trip

I ... case: it is not quite clear what Mowbray means here: probably he intends Henry and the court to understand that he failed in his duty because he did not manage to save Gloucester (which is, of course, a gross misrepresentation)

ambush: no details are known of this, but that Mowbray should admit this misdemeanour would make him seem honest to the watching nobles

exactly: explicitly

rancour: bitterness, spite

recreant: unchristian

Which ... defend: which charge (that the accusation is groundless spite) I personally will prove

interchangeably:	in return (Mowbray is now accusing, or 'appealing' Henry of treason in his turn)
overwheening:	over-proud
Even ... blood:	that is, by shedding the blood
chambered:	enclosed
In haste whereof:	that his may happen quickly
conclude:	come to an understanding
no month:	through astrology, doctors were thought to know when was the best time of year to treat their patients by bleeding them; throughout this speech Richard plays on the idea of the letting of blood (medicinal bleeding) and blood-letting (fighting)
make-peace:	peace-maker
Throw ... his:	Henry and Mowbray have evidently picked up each other's gages
Obedience ... again:	the obedience a son owes his father demands I should not have to ask again
boot:	remedy
The ... owes:	as a loyal subject ('my duty') I owe you my life ('the one')
my fair ... have:	Mowbray means that Richard shall not command him to submit and so deny him a good name after he is dead
impeached:	accused of treason
baffled:	insulted, disgraced
balm:	healing ointment
breathed ... poison:	uttered this slander
Lions ... tame:	a lion figured in the King's coat of arms, and a leopard in Mowbray's
not ... spots:	the proverb 'The leopard cannot change his spots' derives from the Bible (Jeremiah 13:23)
afford:	offer, allow
That away:	take that away, and
gilded loam:	painted earth
in one:	together
crest-fallen:	humbled
beggar-fear:	that is, fear unbecoming a nobleman
impeach ... height:	disgrace my breeding
outdared:	cowed, that is, overcome by Henry's boldness in accusing him
dastard:	coward
feeble wrong:	cowardly act (as submitting to Mowbray)
sound ... parle:	an image from the blowing (sounding) of trumpets to stop a battle

motive:	organ, that is, his tongue
in his:	to its (that is, the tongue's): the possessive pronoun 'its' did not come into common use until the seventeenth century
St Lambert's Day:	17 September
atone:	reconcile
Justice ... chivalry:	God's justice so guide the courage of the just man that he will be victorious (this was the theory behind trial by combat)
home:	that is, England (as distinct from the troubles abroad in Ireland, of which we hear in I.4.38)
alarms:	troubles, discontents

Act I Scene 2

The matter of this scene is not in the sources of the play: clearly, then, Shakespeare had a particular reason for inventing it and inserting it here. As an intimate and heartfelt dialogue, it does serve to contrast in manner and tone with the pageantry of both I.1 and I.3. However, the crucial point of the scene is that we learn from Gaunt quite definitely that Richard is guilty of Gloucester's death. We are thus in no doubt now that the King, far from being the impartial and just figure he would appear to be, is himself deeply implicated in the quarrel. This will have a bearing on his actions in I.3. This scene also continues the images of blood and the references to Edward III which had been introduced in I.1.

NOTES AND GLOSSARY:

Duchess of Gloucester:	Eleanor Bohun, c.1360–99
part ... blood:	Gaunt and Thomas of Woodstock were brothers
solicit:	tempt
exclaims:	exclamations
But ... correct:	it is the responsibility of Richard, as king, to punish the murderer ('correction') but as he is himself implicated ('which made the fault') there is nothing we can do ('cannot correct')
Put ... heaven:	pray to God to act on our behalf
they:	that is, God and the angels
Finds ... spur:	are you no more anxious than that to act like a brother?
Edward:	Edward III (1327–77), Gaunt's, York's and Thomas's father, and Richard's and Henry's grandfather
seven ... root:	to the image of the vials of blood is added that of a genealogical table or 'tree': Elizabethan tables pla-

	ced the founder of the family at the foot or 'root' (and not at the top, as in a modern table) and showed his descendants as 'branches' of the tree
dried ... course:	have died a natural death of old age
by ... cut:	died violently, as in battle
envy:	hatred
mettle:	stuff
self:	same
Yet ... him:	part of you is killed too, as you share his blood (and, the Duchess implies, you are therefore concerned and should act on his behalf)
Thou ... life:	the same thought as in lines 24–5: since Edward's blood was in Thomas's veins, Gaunt's acceptance of Thomas's murder is acceptance of the death of his own father
patience:	the Christian virtue of accepting humbly whatever God brings to pass
despair:	the sin of supposing God cannot help us and that there is nothing to be done to better our condition
suffering:	allowing
In ... life:	the Duchess appeals to Gaunt's self-interest: to allow the murderer to escape is to risk his own life (see lines 35–6)
mean:	ordinary, common
venge:	avenge
God's substitute:	the King, thought to be divinely appointed (see Richard's view in III.2 54–62, III.3.72–81, and the Bishop of Carlisle's in IV.1.121–9)
I ... minister:	it was accepted in the Elizabethan period that no subject could judge or rebel against a true king (see the references above)
Where ... myself:	to whom, then, may I complain?
cousin:	used loosely by Elizabethans to mean 'relative'
fell:	cruel, ruthless
if ... career:	if Mowbray is not killed with the first charge
courser:	horse
lists:	the ground between the spectators where the combatants would fight
caitiff recreant:	captive coward
Thy sometimes:	she who was formerly your
boundeth:	rebounds
Not ... weight:	a ball bounces because it is hollow, but, by contrast, her grief rebounds because it is so heavy with sadness

Pleshey:	Thomas of Woodstock had a country house in this Essex village
lodgings:	rooms
offices:	servants' quarters
Therefore ... me:	since York would find only sorrow at Pleshey the Duchess decides not to invite him to come, but merely asks Gaunt to commend her to him
The last leave:	that is, she expects to die of grief (as occurs, II.2.97) and so will not see him again

Act I Scene 3

After the pause of I.2, we return to the pageantry of I.1, now in no doubt as to Richard's involvement in this affair. It is 17 September 1398 and the lists have been prepared at Coventry for the trial by combat, to which Richard had finally agreed, to see whether Mowbray is the traitor Henry claims (I.1.196–205). Shakespeare, following Holinshed closely, gives full weight to the formal splendour of the occasion: the scene builds up tension slowly through the chivalric formalities of the identification of the combatants, the statement of the cause of the quarrel and the swearing of oaths, the ceremonial leave-takings, the arming of the combatants and the final declaration by the heralds until, at last, the Lord Marshal orders the trumpets to sound to begin the contest. At this moment, Richard intervenes and stops the fight. This sudden, unexpected, turn of events is very dramatic, precisely because Shakespeare has so carefully prepared us to expect something quite different.

But why does Richard intervene, stop the fight, and banish both Henry and Mowbray, when (as he himself had said, I.1.25–7) one of them must be innocent? Some critics find here evidence of Richard's wilfulness, his unstable nature and tendency to rule in an irrational and arbitrary fashion. That Richard, on the spur of the moment, later reduces the length of Henry's banishment (lines 208–11) seems to support the view that he acts from mere whim, enjoying his power in an irresponsible way. Henry's comment (lines 213–15) underlines this arbitrary power, and Gaunt's reply (lines 216–32) looks very much like a pointed rebuke showing Richard that he is not, after all, all powerful— he cannot keep Gaunt young.

It is, however, possible to take another view of this event, namely, that Richard is, in fact, very much in control, and makes here a master-stroke of policy. We have seen that this quarrel concerns him intimately: both Mowbray (as his agent in the murder) and Henry (who seeks to redress this wrong) pose a threat to him. Richard himself detects ambition in them (lines 129–32) and is anxious that they should not conspire together against him (lines 178–90). By banishing both, he not only removes both threats but retains the appearance of impartiality. Had they fought, the victor, whichever it might be, would have been in a very strong position to challenge Richard—Mowbray by threatening to reveal the truth, Henry by questioning Richard's own part in Gloucester's death. So Richard could be said to be preserving his own power in a cunning way by his intervention before either man has proved his innocence. Of course the plan (if such it be) does not work: but that Richard is, in some respects, a rather nasty character, capable of such deviousness, will appear in the very next scene. Why, though, Henry should be banished for a shorter period than Mowbray is not clear, whichever view we take of Richard's action. It may be we are to suppose that Henry's popularity means that were Richard to act too severely against him there would be a risk of popular rebellion in his support, but the evidence for this popularity only comes later (I.4.23–36).

The scene ends with remarkable dignity and nobility in the responses of both men to their king's treatment of them, and Gaunt's expression of grief. It is very difficult not to feel that all three behave themselves with more real nobility than Richard.

NOTES AND GLOSSARY:

Duke of Aumerle: Edward of Norwich (c.1373–1415), York's eldest son (and so Henry's cousin, line 64), is to play a significant part in the fifth act: here, he serves the Lord Marshal as High Constable; his noble and brave death at the battle of Agincourt is remembered in *Henry V*, IV.6.3–34

at all points: completely

enter in: the stage itself is imagined as the lists, the field of combat, to which the appellants enter from either side; the audience of the play thus finds itself in the actual position of spectators at the trial

sprightfully ... bold: eagerly and boldly

Stays but: only waits for

Bushy ... Green: Sir John Bushy (or Bussy), Sir William Bagot and Sir Henry Green were councillors who actively promoted Richard's policies in Parliament: in the play they are less important as individuals than as representatives of the favourites who ill-advised Richard and reaped personal gain from his corrupt rule; Bushy and Green were executed at Bristol in 1399 by the supporters of Henry (III.1.1–35), Bagot escaped to Ireland and died in 1407, but there is some confusion over Bagot in this play, see notes on pages 52, 57 and 66

orderly … cause:	proceed in due order to have him swear that his cause is just
say … art:	the formal identification of combatants was necessary since a knight in full armour with his visor down would not be recognisable
what … quarrel:	what is the cause of your complaint
As … valour:	so that heaven and your valour may defend you
defend:	forbid
truth:	the word conveys more than mere honesty: integrity, loyalty, trustworthiness and nobility are all implied, for to be 'true' was the mark of the chivalric knight
my … issue:	Mowbray defends the good name of his descendants who would be ashamed to have an ancestor who was a traitor
truly:	on behalf of the truth
plated … war:	enclosed in plate armour
Depose … in:	swear him to
daring-hardy:	foolishly bold, reckless
Appointed:	as are appointed
fair designs:	noble undertakings
blood:	that is, kinsman
Lament … dead:	should Henry die, no man could avenge his death as by it he would have proved his guilt
profane:	waste by shedding needlessly
lusty:	vigorous, full of life
cheerly:	happily, but stronger in sense than its modern equivalent: there is a suggestion of boldness, bravery
regreet:	welcome
daintiest last:	English feasts ended with sweet confections
regenerate:	reborn
two fold:	because Henry enjoys both his own youth and that of his father reborn in him (line 70)
proof:	'proof armour' was armour whose strength had been proved in combat; Henry is asking his father to give this guarantee of strength to his own armour by his prayers
steel:	harden
That … coat:	so that it may pierce Mowbray's coat of mail as if it were soft as wax
furbish:	literally, to clean and polish armour: Henry means that his success would give new brilliance to the name of John of Gaunt

haviour:	behaviour
amazing:	stunning (the word had a much stronger sense then than now)
casque:	helmet
However ... gentlemen:	an understandable boast, but not one the theory of trial by combat would support: the defeated party was adjudged guilty
enfranchisement:	freedom, liberation
More:	that is, no freed captive was ever more joyous than he at the prospect of this combat
feast:	festivity (in keeping with 'freer heart', 'dancing soul', 'jocund')
jest:	sport
Securely ... eye:	either Richard is confident ('securely') of the virtue and valour he sees in Mowbray's face, or he sees virtue and valour confidently lying ('couched') within Mowbray's eyes—the latter is perhaps more likely, since Mowbray's last speech had indeed been confident
Receive ... lance:	combatants did not bring their own lances but received them from the Marshal who could ensure that they were of equal length
Strong ... hope:	a biblical phrase from Psalms 61:3
On ... false:	on pain of being himself found false (if he fails to defeat Mowbray)
approve:	prove
Attending:	waiting for
set forward:	it is just possible horses were actually used in the Elizabethan theatre
warder:	ceremonial staff or baton
chairs:	after formally identifying himself, a knight at an actual trial would sit in a ceremonial chair within a small tent or pavilion until the contest was to begin; it may be that chairs were placed on either side of Shakespeare's stage
While we return:	until we inform
flourish:	trumpet call
council:	those noblemen intimate with the King would form his council of advisors
For that:	so that
dire aspect:	awful appearance
set on you:	set you on
Which:	the syntax of the passage is confused: 'which' seems to refer to 'peace' (line 132), but, if so, then peace,

having been 'roused up' (line 134) goes on to 'fright fair peace' (line 137), which makes little sense; some critics feel the confusion indicates that Richard is hiding his true motives (see scene summary), but there is probably textual corruption here (the passage is omitted from the Folio text); the general thrust (that this combat might lead to further conflict and so permanently endanger peace) is clear

bray:	sound, cry
arms:	weapons
you our:	you from our
upon ... life:	upon pain of forfeiting your life (if he returns before the term is up)
regreet:	greet again
stranger:	foreign (not a comparative adjective here)
point on:	aim at
determine:	put an end to
dateless limit:	endless term, limitless extent
dear:	dreadful, dire
A ... maim:	a better reward and not so deep an injury
forty years:	Mowbray was in fact thirty-three years old in 1398
And ... more:	either 'and now my tongue is no more use to me' or 'and now the use of my tongue is (mine) no more'
viol:	stringed musical instrument played with a bow, the predecessor of the violin
Or ... up:	or like an instrument capable of producing subtle sounds shut up in its box silent and useless
That ... touch:	who does not know how to play it
portcullis:	heavy metal grid which could be lowered to seal off the entrance to a castle
And ... me:	Mowbray's ignorance of foreign languages will prevent him from talking (and so is the gaoler of his tongue)
I ... nurse:	learn a new language as would a child from its wet-nurse
speechless death:	the dead are silent, and as Mowbray will no more speak his native language, his exile will be a death
It ... compassionate:	either 'it is no use being sorry for yourself' or 'it is no use asking for pity'
plaining:	complaining
on ... sword:	where the blade and hilt of a sword join the hand guard a cross is formed, so an oath sworn on a sword is sworn on the supreme symbol of Christianity
Our part:	that is, the duty you owe me as God's deputy

lowering:	glowering
advised purpose:	arrangement, plan
so ... enemy:	so much I can say to my enemy
frail ... flesh:	weak tomb (of the soul) made of flesh
book of life:	it was thought that the names of those to enjoy the bliss of Heaven were written in God's book (Revelation 3:5)
rue:	this small word suggests a good deal: the meaning is that when Richard himself comes, through cruel experience, to discover what Henry is really like, he will bitterly regret it
Now ... way:	either 'I am free to wander anywhere in the world ("all the world's my way") and so cannot go astray ("stray") unless I return to England ("Save back ...")', or 'I cannot go astray now for, with the exception of returning to England, I am free to wander anywhere in the world'; the punctuation of the Penguin edition favours the latter reading
glasses:	mirrors (since they reflect Gaunt's feelings)
lagging:	slow
wanton:	rich, luxuriant
in ... me:	out of regard or consideration to me
vantage:	advantage
change ... moons:	that is, can pass (the years being measured by the waxing and the waning of the moon rather than by the earth's movement round the sun)
bring ... about:	complete the length of time
oil, dried lamp:	a lamp without oil would not, of course, light
time-bewasted:	wasted by time
extinct:	extinguished
inch of taper:	a 'taper' is a candle: Gaunt likens the short period of life left to him to the last inch of a candle before it burns out
blindfold death:	Shakespeare here perhaps personifies death, which was frequently pictured as blind (the traditional symbol of death, a skull, is, of course, eyeless): however, the phrase may be read in many ways, none necessarily exclusive: death is 'blind' because it is impartial, visiting noblemen and common people alike; death does 'blindfold' the dead since they no longer see this world; and, in this instance, for Gaunt, death would be the blindfold preventing him from seeing his son
furrow:	wrinkle

pilgrimage:	journey, passage (of time)
current:	valid, acceptable
tongue ... gave:	your voice contributed to the discussion which led to our decision
smooth:	mitigate, excuse, gloss over
partial slander:	the accusation of being biased in Henry's favour
And ... destroyed:	and in the sentence of banishment to which I agreed I destroyed my own life
looked when:	expected that, waited for
to ... own:	in making my own son
What ... know:	what we shall not be able to learn from you personally (since Henry will be in exile)
Cousin ... show:	as Aumerle accompanies Henry (I.4.3–4) it is odd that he should here take his leave of him
let ... show:	that is, write in a letter
My ... side:	it is curious that the Duke of Surrey, who acted as Lord Marshal on this occasion (see note at the beginning of I.1), should be so friendly to Henry when he appears later (IV.1.60–71) as a supporter of Richard: it may be that Shakespeare either did not know, or had forgotten, that the Lord Marshal *was* the Duke of Surrey, and so thought of the two figures as two distinct characters, which is how they are listed in the *dramatis personae* in most modern editions
too few:	that is, too few words
prodigal:	liberal, lavish
To breathe:	in expressing
grief:	both 'sorrow' and 'cause for sorrow'
sullen:	sad
foil ... set:	Gaunt means that Henry's homecoming will be the happier when set against the sadness of his exile
remember ... world:	remind me what a distance
jewels:	that is, the things and people he most values
apprenticehood:	apprenticeship
passages:	experiences
Must ... grief?:	Henry will, like an apprentice, learn the ways of foreign travel and having mastered them like a journeyman (a qualified craftsman), when his exile is over (to 'have freedom' was the technical term for the end of an apprenticeship) he will not, like a true journeyman, be proud of the achievement but will see it merely as an undesirably full acquaintance with sorrow

All ... necessity:	proverbial wisdom, that, since all the earth is God's, one can never be truly banished as it is impossible to leave his sight and so the proper course is to benefit from whatever circumstances we find ourselves in
necessity:	that is, what you have to do against your will
faintly:	faint-heartedly, unwillingly
purchase:	gain
Devouring pestilence:	plague
Look what:	whatever
presence:	the presence chamber where the monarch received visitors
strewed:	covered (the floors of rooms were covered with rushes)
measure:	dance
gnarling:	snarling
Caucasus:	mountain range in southern Russia dividing Europe from Asia
cloy:	stifle by over-indulging
fantastic:	imaginary
apprehension:	conception, knowledge
worse:	that is, those things we experience worse than the good we know could be ours
Fell ... sore:	in line 292 sorrow had been conceived of as a snarling animal which bites, and that metaphor is continued here: cruel ('Fell') sorrow's teeth make the most festering wounds ('doth never rankle more') when he bites but does not make a deep wound like that a surgeon cuts ('lanceth') to cure a poisoned abscess ('sore'): Henry seems to feel that the bitterness of sorrow can (like a surgeon's knife which cuts sharply to heal) be its own cure if it is recognised for what it is, and that Gaunt, by offering weak consolation, threatens not to end Henry's sorrow but only to dull it (or blunt the surgeon's knife) so that it will linger on and on

Act I Scene 4

As Shakespeare had varied the dramatic pace and tone by following the court scene of 1.1 with the private anguish of 1.2, so now the pageantry of 1.3 is followed by a very different kind of scene. Suddenly, we are taken 'behind the scenes' of such a formal state occasion as we have just witnessed, and we see Richard as he is when he is not acting the King before an audience. It is a shocking sight. All his nobility of manner and fine eloquence has gone. As we hear him talk in confidence to his closest friends we learn that he is intensely resentful of Henry's popularity with the common people. The scornful way in which Richard speaks of his common subjects makes it perfectly clear that he will do nothing to win or deserve their affection. Henry, as Richard recognises, has already usurped Richard's place in the people's hearts: no wonder there had been hints earlier that Richard feared him (I.1.109, I.3.129–33), or that Richard banished him. There may even be a suggestion that Richard does not intend that he shall ever return (lines 20–2). We then learn that, to finance his expedition against the Irish rebels, Richard plans to use unjust and tyrannical methods, giving his favourites power to raise taxes for themselves in return for ready money and forcing wealthy subjects to give him large sums of money. Finally (and, perhaps, most shockingly), we discover that his consideration to Gaunt in I.3.208–11 was sheer hypocrisy. When, at the end of the scene, Richard learns that Gaunt is dying, he speaks of him with horrible callousness, hoping he will die soon so that his wealth can be seized.

This is only a short scene, but it is a splendid example of how much Shakespeare can achieve in a short space. Building on earlier hints and suspicions he now suddenly and graphically reveals the King for what he is. We begin to feel that no such king can survive long.

NOTES AND GLOSSARY:

We ... observe:	Richard enters in the midst of conversation; the topic appears later, at line 24
high:	both high-ranking or noble and proud and haughty
for me:	by me
rheum:	watery fluid
grace:	that is, here, give a fitting show of emotions to
hollow:	Aumerle is much colder towards Henry than in I.3.249–50: the irony of line 3 suggests he does not consider Henry noble, and now he claims their parting was 'hollow' (that is, without true sorrow) and any tears the result not of feeling but of the cold wind
craft:	cunning skill
To counterfeit ... grave:	pretend to be so afflicted by grief that words were as impossible to utter as if they had been buried in a grave made by sorrow
'tis doubt:	it is doubtful
Whether ... friends:	Richard means by 'friends' noble relatives: it is doubtful whether Henry will see them when he returns because, as Richard goes on sarcastically to explain, Henry seems to prefer the common people;

	there may also be the more sinister implication that it is 'doubtful' whether Henry will visit his friends when his term is up because Richard does not intend that he will ever be allowed to return—the possibility that Richard intends to have him murdered cannot be excluded
slaves:	not literally 'slaves', but a term of contempt for common people
underbearing:	endurance
As ... him:	as if he were trying to take into exile ('banish') the affections ('affects') of the people with him
oyster-wench:	woman who sells oysters
draymen:	men who drive large horse-drawn carts (or 'drays')
And ... knee:	that is, Henry bends his knee to them in a curtsey (not then confined to women)
our:	that is, Richard's (*not* Richard's and Aumerle's)
reversion:	a legal term for the return of property to its rightful owner on the death of a tenant
next degree in:	next object of (upon Richard's death)
go ... thoughts:	let these thoughts go too
stand out:	resist
Expedient manage:	quick and efficient arrangements
too ... court:	that is, maintaining the court on too lavish a scale
largess:	bounty, generosity
farm:	in return for an immediate sum of money Richard will make over to certain people the revenues and taxes due to him as king: thus to yield up his power over large areas of his realm in return for money was wickedly irresponsible in a king—it meant *he* no longer ruled
substitutes:	deputies, officers
blank charters:	legal documents wealthy subjects were made to sign by which they promised to pay the King unspecified sums of money; the King (or his agents) wrote in whatever figure they thought fit *after* the document was signed
presently:	immediately
taken:	fallen ill
post-haste:	as quickly as possible
Ely House:	the palace of the Bishop of Ely at Holborn, near London
lining:	Richard means, of course, the contents, which 'line' Gaunt's treasure chests ('coffers'); the word fits with the 'coats' that follow

Act II Scene 1

This long scene concludes the first movement of the play and begins the second. It is crucial to the action for it draws together and confirms all we have learned about Richard as king and shows him making a decision (to seize Gaunt's wealth) which will be the immediate cause of his downfall. This is our last sight of Richard as unchallenged king, for, after the exits (line 223), we do not see him again until the balance of power has shifted decisively to Henry. The scene is made up of three events:

(1) The death of Gaunt. There is no clue for the opening of the scene in Shakespeare's sources nor for the dignity, wisdom and nobility he gives to Gaunt: his 'England' speech is entirely Shakespeare's invention. It is not, however, difficult to see why Shakespeare chose to introduce the incident. The scene begins by stressing Richard's youthful folly more strongly than has yet been done by having the old and experienced noble princes, York and Gaunt, speak despairingly of him. In Gaunt's very famous prophetic speech (lines 31–68) there is a superb expression of patriotic devotion to that England Richard threatens to destroy. In fact, Shakespeare here conveys far more than one man's particular affection for his country: the speech celebrates the patriotic fervour which runs through all the history plays and gives a moving poetic vision of that England which, finally, triumphs in the Tudors over all the wars and treacheries which follow Richard's death. Hearing it, the Elizabethan would hear *his* England described. More especially, the speech highlights the negligence of Richard in failing to rule such a kingdom well. Richard's failings as king become still more apparent when he enters (line 69) for Gaunt rebukes him for: (*i*) submitting himself to the evil influence of flatterers, (*ii*) shaming the noble blood of Edward III and killing his descendants, and (*iii*) leasing out his land in return for money.

(2) The seizure of Gaunt's wealth and York's protest. Gaunt leaves the stage (line 138) and in a moment we hear he has died. Triumphantly, Richard immediately plans to seize his wealth to finance his Irish campaign. York, Gaunt's brother and now 'the last of noble Edward's sons' (line 171), endeavours to dissuade the King from thus depriving Henry Bolingbroke of his inheritance. He points out that Richard himself holds his throne by the laws of inheritance: to deny Henry his birthright is to deny his own title to the crown and is to undercut the very foundations of society. And York foretells terrible consequences if Richard goes ahead with his scheme (lines 189–98). Richard, however, pays no attention, and leaves determined to set out for Ireland the next day, making York governor of England in his absence.

(3) The beginning of Richard's downfall. When the King has left, three noblemen remain on stage and rehearse to each other the wrongs which they and England have endured under Richard. After some persuasion, Northumberland reveals that Henry is ready to sail from France with an invasion force, and is only waiting for Richard to leave for Ireland before setting out. The three agree to meet him at the port of Ravenspurgh. As yet it is not clear just what Henry hopes to gain by invading England: there is only a general feeling he comes to right his own, and perhaps England's, wrongs. The decision of these noblemen and the hints we had in I.4 of popular support for Henry prepare us to expect that Henry will not be resisted and that Richard will quickly be deserted by any followers. So begins the King's fall.

Thus, in this scene Richard's failings are stressed by Gaunt, York and the three noblemen, and we see that he is going to pay for ignoring his people, refusing good counsel and ruling illegally. Events seem to move very fast: all this seems to come immediately after Henry's banishment. In fact, Shakespeare has telescoped events together to give this effect. Henry was banished in September 1398; Gaunt died in February 1399; Richard did not leave for Ireland until three months later, in May 1399, and Henry landed in July. There is no sense of this passage of time in the play. It all happens too quickly to be realistic: how could Henry have already organised an invasion force? In any case, as it is only in this scene that Richard decides to deny him his rights, he could not yet possibly know about it. But dramatically it gives the impression that events are now taking control and that Richard is helpless to prevent them.

NOTES AND GLOSSARY:

Duke of York:	Edmund of Langley (1341–1402), fifth son of Edward III, and so Gaunt's brother, uncle to Richard and Henry, and Aumerle's father: his descendants (the Yorkists) were to fight Gaunt's descendants (the Lancastrians) for the English crown
Earl of Northumberland:	Sir Henry Percy (1342–1408), father of Harry Percy (the Hotspur of *1 Henry IV*); he played a leading part in Henry's gaining of the throne, only to rebel against him later
unstaid:	uncontrolled, unrestrained
listened more:	listened to more attentively
glose:	flatter
close:	the conclusion of a piece of music
As ... last:	either 'as the final taste of a sweet thing is sweetest because it is last' or 'the final taste of a sweet thing is sweetest because, being the last, it lingers longest'

death's ... tale:	serious dying words
the wise:	even the wise (and so much more the foolish Richard)
lascivious metres:	wanton verse
Italy:	Elizabethan writers habitually attributed all kinds of bad influence to Italy
tardy-apish:	that is, the English imitate a fashion when it is already out of date
variety:	silly, inconsequential thing
Where ... regard:	when the will (or inclination) over-rules the advice of the understanding
Tis ... lose:	a poor quibble to modern taste: to advise Richard is (as we still say) a waste of breath, and Gaunt has little enough to spare ('lackest') both because, as he is ill, he has difficulty breathing and is short of breath, and because, as he is dying, he has only a few more breaths to draw
Methinks ... inspired:	the idea that, in their dying moments, men might become prophetic, was common (see lines 5–6)
expiring:	dying, but the pun on 'breath' continues: by breathing in ('inspiring') Gaunt has gained breath which he now breathes out ('expires') in what follows
riot:	indulgent and extravagant way of life
betimes, betimes:	'soon', and, at the end of the line, 'early in the day'
Light ... means:	a frivolous way of life, like a gluttonous cormorant consuming everything
earth of majesty:	this land which is best suited to majesty
seat of Mars:	as Mars was the Roman god of war the suggestion is that England is famous for military bravery
Eden:	the paradise in which the first man and woman, Adam and Eve, lived until their fall from God's favour (Genesis 3:23–4)
demi-paradise:	one of two paradises (rather than half a paradise)
infection:	evil foreign influences
envy:	hatred, hostility
teeming:	fertile
Feared ... breed:	inspiring fear by the nobility of their breeding
by their birth:	on account of their noble birth
For ... chivalry:	this line enlarges on 'deeds' in line 53, and so the phrase 'as far from home' (line 53) more naturally follows it: their deeds (line 53) of Christian service (that is, the Crusades) and chivalry (line 54) are renowned as far from home (line 53) as is Christ's tomb (line 55)

sepulchre:	the tomb in which Christ was laid after the Crucifixion and from which he rose from the dead (Luke 23:50–24:12)
stubborn Jewry:	the Jews are stubborn because they refuse to be converted to Christianity
world's ransom:	Christians believe Christ died for the sins of the whole world, that is, his death frees men from the punishment due to their sin as the payment of a ransom freed a captive taken in war (1 Timothy 2:6)
Mary's son:	Christ
tenement:	estate held by a tenant
pelting:	paltry, insignificant
Neptune:	the Roman god of the sea
risky ... bonds:	the blank charters mentioned in I.4.58
Queen Isabel:	Richard married his second wife, Isabella (1389–1409), daughter of Charles V of France, in 1396, when she was only eight years old, but in Shakespeare's play she is a mature woman: she returned to France in 1401
Ross, and Willoughby:	noblemen who died in 1414 and 1409 respectively: they changed their allegiance to Henry
raged:	it seems rather pointless to say that young horses rage the more when they are 'raged': some editors therefore change 'raged' to 'rein'd', which makes sense (young horses, if restrained, get more angry) and fits with York's argument that the young king is best not rebuked
composition:	state of being, constitution, the condition I am in
gaunt:	grown thin and drawn with age
tedious fast:	painful and long fast
watched:	three senses mingle: looked at (England's state), been kept awake (by worry) and kept a vigil
Watching:	sleeplessness
The pleasure ... looks:	Gaunt means that, as he is denied the pleasure of his son Henry, he abstains (or fasts) from what most fathers enjoy
inherits:	possesses
nicely:	both subtly or cleverly and foolishly
kill ... me:	by banishing his heir, in whom his name would live after his death (Gaunt, of course, does not know Richard intends to kill his name more completely still by denying Henry his inheritance)
flatter:	that is, in order to cheer up

he ... me:	God
I ... ill:	Gaunt uses the word in two senses: I cannot see you well ('ill' in the sense of 'badly', because Gaunt himself is ill) and I see that *you* are ill
Ill ... ill:	it makes me ill to see you, and in you I see evil
Thy ... land:	your land is itself your death-bed
careless patient:	careless as a patient
'physicians' ... thee:	that is, Richard's circle of favourites, the flatterers of line 100
no ... than:	no less than the whole of
grandsire:	Edward III
son's son:	Richard
sons:	Gloucester and Gaunt
possessed:	(in line 107) in possession of (your kingdom); (in line 108) determined
regent:	ruler
But ... land:	but as you enjoy only this land (and not the whole world) as your kingdom
Thy ... law:	Gaunt means that as Richard has let out his land for money he is no longer its king, the source of law, but a landlord subject, like any other, to the common laws of the land
ague:	fever
native:	natural
seat:	throne
great ... son:	Edward the Black Prince, Richard's father
roundly:	bluntly or glibly; either sense may be intended
Should ... shoulders:	that is, were Gaunt not of royal blood his words would deserve execution as punishment
irreverent:	disrespectful
Edward:	(in line 124) the Black Prince; (in line 125) Edward III
pelican:	the young pelican was thought to feed on the blood of its parents
tapped out:	let out
fair befall:	may good come to
unkindness:	unnatural behaviour
crooked:	bent double
sullens:	sulks
become:	are fit for, suit
Harry:	Henry Bolingbroke
As ... his:	Richard means neither Gaunt nor Henry bear him any love
His ... be:	his life is over, ours is still before us
supplant:	remove

rug ... kerns:	long-haired Irish soldiers
where ... live:	according to legend St Patrick, patron saint of Ireland, drove all snakes from the island
plate:	gold and silver plates, cups and dishes
Gaunt's rebukes:	the rebukes given to Gaunt by Richard (*not* vice versa)
private wrongs:	wrongs suffered by ordinary citizens
Nor ... marriage:	Richard prevented Henry's intended marriage, as Holinshed records, but this is not mentioned elsewhere in the play
bend ... wrinkle:	frown
Accomplished ... hours:	when he was your age
His ... won:	an allusion to the fact that, unlike his father, Richard had had no military successes (which would have brought tribute, taxes and ransoms into the treasury)
compare between:	that is, make a comparison between Richard and his father, the Black Prince
royalties:	rights granted by the King, titles
charters ... rights:	agreements and traditional laws of inheritance
God ... true:	God forbid that what I say should come to pass
Call ... livery:	under feudal law, upon a nobleman's death his lands became the property of the King until the heir proved himself to be true heir and of age: the letters patents were issued by the King to allow the heir to have lawyers ('attorneys general') go through the legal process of inheriting his father's lands and titles ('sue his livery'), and so, by revoking them ('Call in') Richard would prevent Henry from becoming Duke of Lancaster and would himself remain in control of the Lancastrian wealth
deny ... homage:	an heir received his inheritance on condition he made an act of homage to the King: to refuse ('deny') homage from Henry would thus be to refuse him his inheritance
thoughts ... think:	that is, thoughts of disobedience and rebellion unbecoming a loyal subject
But ... good:	we may be sure ('understood') that the consequences ('events') of bad actions ('courses') can never be ('fall out') good
Earl of Wiltshire:	William Le Scrope (1351?–99), Richard's treasurer, executed with Bushy and Green (III.2.122–42), but he does not appear in the play
repair to:	come to

Ely House:	where Richard now is (I.4.57)
time ... trow:	high time I believe
in ... ourself:	while I am away
liberal:	free, unrestrained (Ross is afraid to speak his mind lest his words be reported to Richard)
Tends ... speak:	has what you would say to do with
Bereft ... patrimony: denied and deprived of his inheritance
Merely in:	simply out of
prosecute:	act upon
pilled:	robbed, plundered
exactions:	extortions
blanks, benevolences: blank charters (I.4.48) and forced loans
wot:	know
this:	that is, the money raised by the loans and other devices
compromise:	that is, a compromise peace treaty
sore:	dangerously
strike:	strike or take down sail (that is, take precautions) with a pun on 'strike' in the sense strike or fight back
securely:	carelessly, over-confidently
wrack:	shipwreck
suffering:	tolerating
hollow eyes:	the eye-sockets of a skull
are but thyself:	are one with you, agree with you
Le Port Blanc:	a port on the French coast of Brittany (the Brittaine of line 278)
Rainold ... Brittaine: who these figures were matters less to an audience than the effect of large scale support for Henry which the list gives; they are all taken direct from Holinshed and none appears in the play
broke:	escaped
expedience:	speed
touch:	land on
Imp:	repair (a word used in falconry)
broking pawn:	pawn-brokers, money-lenders
Ravenspurgh:	a port in England on the river Humber
Hold ... horse:	if my horse can hold out (that is, riding at speed)

Act II Scene 2

This scene confirms the tragic turn of events hinted at in II.1. That scene had ended with the ominous news of Henry's force. Richard has now left for Ireland (lines 4, 41–5) and Henry, who had only been waiting for this (II.1.289–90), has now landed in England (lines 46–51). This is all the scene adds to the plot, but it makes a much larger contribution to the play in the way it affects our view of Richard and his fortunes:

(*i*) The Queen is naturally sad at being parted from Richard, but she struggles too with a 'nameless woe', a dread of she knows not what, something in the future—and then we learn that Henry has landed. This gives a note of foreboding: something terrible is to happen.

(*ii*) In showing the Queen's love and concern for Richard the scene begins the very important process whereby, after seeing Richard's rather sordid dealings in I.4 and II.1, our sympathy is aroused for him. To the Queen (and so for the audience) he is a man, not a scheming tyrant.

(*iii*) The death of the Duchess of Gloucester deepens the atmosphere of gloom, but, more significantly, it stresses the helplessness of York. He is governor of England (II.1.219–20), but he has little hope of resisting Henry (line 87). He had hoped to ask his sister-in-law for money (lines 90–1) but her death prevents this and, by adding to his sorrow, only makes him more perplexed. He is stunned: 'I know not what to do' (line 100). We knew York was a mild man because he had tried to dissuade Gaunt from speaking out in II.1; it now appears he is quite unfit to protect Richard's interests. Not only is he impractical, but he has much sympathy for Henry (lines 109–15). Already it seems Richard's position is well-nigh hopeless.

(*iv*) This impression is confirmed at the end of the scene when Richard's favourites desert York (and so Richard's cause) to save their lives. Nobles have left Richard; the common people feel no affection for him (line 88); York is helpless; and now Richard's dearest friends flee. Clearly, the coming of Henry has put all in disarray and there is no one to stop him (line 145–6).

NOTES AND GLOSSARY:

heaviness:	heaviness of spirit, sadness
Save ... farewell:	unless it is that I have said goodbye to
With ... trembles:	trembles with fear although there is no apparent cause
Each ... shadows:	for each real cause of sorrow there are twenty imaginary ones
glazed:	blurred
perspectives:	two senses are used: (*i*) a glass so cut that it reflects many images (the comparison in lines 16–17); (*ii*) a picture so designed that it appears distorted unless viewed from a special and awkward angle (the comparison of lines 18–20)
Distinguish form:	show clear shapes

Looking ... departure: if Bushy were still thinking of the second kind of perspective this would give a true picture; as he is arguing the Queen sees more causes of sorrow than there actually are (line 22), he appears to have returned to the comparison with the first kind of perspective, but the passage is confusing: the main point to grasp is the distinction between real and imaginary causes of sorrow

Find: finds ('your sweet majesty' of line 20 is the subject)

Which ... is: which shapes of grief, looked on as they are, are

Which ... imaginary: which, instead of weeping because of true things, weeps for imaginary ones

though ... think: though I am thinking on nothing melancholy ('thought')

conceit: imagination, fancy (Bushy implies it is no *more* than imaginary, hence the Queen's reply in line 34)

Mine ... wot: the wordplay now becomes very teasing: we might paraphrase the sense 'My grief is not mere fancy, for either an imaginary cause of sorrow ("nothing", line 36) has resulted in ("begot") my real sorrow ("something grief"), or there is an actual cause of grief ("something", line 37) which, though I do not know what it is, would actually justify the sorrow ("nothing") which I feel ("grieve")—if so, it is mine because I feel it, even though its cause as yet belongs elsewhere (line 38)—I cannot give a name to what is not yet known: "nameless woe" would, I suppose, be the best way to describe it'

his haste: in his haste lies

retired ... power: brought back his armed forces

revolted faction: the party of rebels

Earl of Worcester: Sir Thomas Percy (1344?–1403), brother of Northumberland; he does not appear in this play but has a significant part in *1 Henry IV*

staff: the symbol of Thomas Percy's office of steward of the royal household

prodigy: unnatural thing, monstrous child

cozening: cheating, deceitful

parasite: a creature that lives off others

bands: bonds

lingers in extremity: prolongs as long as possible

signs ... neck: York wears a piece of neck armour

belie: be false to, misrepresent

crosses: frustrations, troubles

far off:	what lies far away (that is, Ireland)
underprop:	support
surfeit:	extravagance
son:	Aumerle, who had gone to Ireland with Richard
Go ... will:	let things go on as they will (a resigned comment from a man with little hope of changing the course of events)
revolt on:	rebel with
Pleshey:	Gloucester's country house (I.2.66)
sister Gloucester:	sister-in-law, the Duchess of Gloucester
knave:	fellow (with no contemptuous overtone)
God ... mercy:	a common exclamation
I ... God:	I wish, in God's name
So ... it:	as long as my loyalty was not the cause
brother:	Gloucester
posts:	messengers
for:	to
How:	what
sister ... cousin:	York addresses the Queen, his cousin or kinswoman (by her marriage to Richard), but the death of the Duchess is uppermost in his mind and so, thinking of her, he says 'sister' by mistake
Never ... me:	do not believe me if I say it
dispose:	find a place for you to go to
uneven:	confused
The ... returns:	that is, the wind is in the right direction to blow ships to Ireland, but not from it
levy:	raise
Proportionable:	equal
Is ... of:	means that we are hated by
office:	service
presages:	fears for the future
thrives ... beat:	succeeds in driving

Act II Scene 3

The turning of fortune's wheel, which began at the end of II.1 and was so clear in II.2, now accelerates. Henry is making his way through Gloucestershire in the company of Northumberland (who had met him at Ravenspurgh, II.1.296). As he does so, he meets no opposition and is joined by a steady succession of supporters—Harry Percy, Ross and Willoughby. When he comes to Berkeley Castle, held by York, there is still no opposition. Henry claims that he has come only to secure his rights as Duke of Lancaster (and we know York has much sympathy for the justice of his claim, II.1.189–99, II.2.111–15). York, while he cannot approve Henry's breaking of the law in returning to England with an army, admits he has no power to stop him, and so withdraws from the contest, claiming to be neutral. Nevertheless, he invites Henry to spend the night with him at the castle, and we learn Henry intends to go on to Bristol where two of Richard's favourites are in hiding.

The thing to notice is the *ease* of this invasion: Henry rides through England not like an outlaw and rebel but like a hero welcomed by all he meets. Dramatically this confirms our impression that there is no support for Richard and that he is doomed.

NOTES AND GLOSSARY:

in:	by
beguiled:	eased
process:	progress
Harry Percy:	Sir Henry Percy (1364–1403), son of the Earl of Northumberland, who, as Hotspur, plays an important role in the rebellion of the Percys against Henry covered in *1 Henry IV*: despite the 'boy' of line 36 and his protestations of youth (line 42) he was in fact older than Henry who was born in 1367
whencesoever:	wherever he is
tender, raw:	young, inexperienced
gentle:	noble
As ... remembering:	as in having a heart which remembers
It ... recompense:	it shall constantly ('still') reward ('recompense') your true love
covenant:	undertaking, bond
stir Keeps:	arrangements makes
tuft:	clump, copse
Bloody ... spurring:	that is, they have made their horses bleed by pricking them with their spurs to urge them on
unfelt:	that is, unfelt by those he would thank since he is not able yet to give them any positive reward
more enriched:	when I am richer
surmounts:	surpasses
Evermore ... poor:	thanks are always what the poor offer
Stands ... bounty:	must take the place of my generosity
'Lancaster':	because Henry is, now that Gaunt is dead, rightfully Duke of Lancaster, a title which takes precedence over Duke of Hereford
raze:	take away
pricks:	spurs, urges
absent time:	time when the King is absent

self-borne:	borne in your own interest (and not your country's)
grace:	usual form of address to a duke
ungracious:	wicked
profane:	blasphemy
more 'why':	more questions
hot:	energetic
palsy:	a complaint, often suffered by the aged, which makes the hands shake
On ... wherein?:	where does it lie in me ('conditions') and in what that I have done
condition:	circumstances
degree:	sort, kind
expiration ... time:	end of your term of banishment
braving:	defiant
for:	to assume the rights of
indifferent:	impartial
upstart:	people of no breeding
unthrifts:	extravagant people
thus:	that is, as Henry has been
To ... bay:	the line uses metaphors from hunting: to 'rouse' is to startle from hiding; the 'bay' is the quarry's last stand after the chase before being killed: the sense is thus 'to seek out his wrongdoers and pursue them until they are caught'
distrained:	seized
challenge law:	what I demand is in the name of the law
It ... upon:	it is up to your grace
endowments:	possessions
kind:	way
Be ... carver:	a colloquial expression meaning to help yourself, decide for yourself (the carver of a joint of meat at table would serve himself)
find ... wrong:	gain the right by doing wrong
abet:	assist
Cherish:	encourage
mend:	present
by ... life:	God
attach:	arrest
neuter:	neutral
Bagot:	Bagot had gone to Ireland (II.2.140), Bushy and Green to Bristol (II.2.134, 136); Shakespeare seems to have confused Bagot with Green here
complices:	accomplices
caterpillars:	parasites

Act II Scene 4

Confronted with such a short scene we may well ask why Shakespeare bothered to include it. It is a question worth asking, for, if we do, we can usually find there is a good reason for this as for every feature of a Shakespeare play. In this case the scene:

(1) Gives the impression of a lapse of time between II.3 and III.1 during which Henry can travel from Berkeley Castle to Bristol.

(2) Intensifies our sense of Richard's predicament by showing yet again supporters deserting him. In this case it is the Welsh army which tires of waiting for his return. We begin to suspect that when he does come back he will be quite alone.

(3) Deepens the mood of ominous foreboding by adding to the prophecies of doom introduced by Gaunt and York in II.1 and continued by the Queen in II.2 (lines 8–15). Salisbury's final speech seems to set the seal on Richard's fate.

NOTES AND GLOSSARY:

Earl of Salisbury:	John Montagu (1350–1400) who, remaining faithful to Richard, takes part in the plot treated in Act V
Welsh Captain:	in Holinshed named as Owen Glendower (1359?–1416?), who took a prominent part in the rebellion against Henry treated in the *Henry IV* plays; there Shakespeare names him, but in this play he is important as representing the general disillusion with Richard, rather than as an individual historical figure, and so is not named
stayed:	waited
And ... together:	that is, hardly managed to keep the Welsh army together
reposeth:	places
bay trees:	an evergreen tree whose leaves were used to make medicine; in art it was a symbol of victory and immortality, so its withering suggests defeat and death
meteors:	falling stars
fixed stars:	in Renaissance astronomy the stars were thought to be fixed in their orbit around the earth
pale ... earth:	the stars and planets were thought to exert an influence on the affairs of men, so 'looks' must be taken in two senses: (*i*) the pale moon appears blood red from the earth, (*ii*) the pale moon exerts a bloody (disastrous) influence over the earth

lean-looked:	lean looking
whisper:	whisper that there will be
signs forerun:	portents announce
firmament:	sky
witnessing:	suggesting
crossly:	contrary

Act III Scene 1

Henry has come to Bristol Castle (as he planned, II.3.163–4) and, having captured Bushy and Green (who had fled there, II.2.134, 136), has them immediately executed. He justifies this by charging them with: (*i*) separating the King from the Queen. There may be a suggestion of homosexuality here, but, if so, it is not developed elsewhere in the play. (*ii*) misrepresenting him to the King, and (*iii*) wronging him by misusing his lands and destroying the symbols of his nobility.

Notice that Shakespeare pays no attention to how Henry took the castle: we do not know whether there was a fight or whether Bushy and Green were easily captured. By ignoring practical points of this kind Shakespeare continues to suggest that Henry's progress is very easy: he actually has to *do* nothing at all.

NOTES AND GLOSSARY:

presently:	immediately
part:	depart from
too ... urging:	too much insisting on
unfold:	reveal, make known
lineaments:	form, natural features
clean:	completely
in manner:	in a manner of speaking
sinful hours:	that is, the many hours during which they kept Richard from his Queen by involving him in extravagant pleasures; there is no hint of separation between Richard and his Queen elsewhere in the play
divorce:	used metaphorically here to mean 'separate'
Broke ... bed:	broke the royal union both enjoyed
misinterpret:	misunderstand
signories:	estates
Disparked:	used for purposes other than the (noble) business of keeping game for hunting
From ... coat:	broken my windows on which was painted my heraldic coat-of-arms
imprese:	heraldic device, badge

sign:	family symbol
dispatched:	executed quickly
intreated:	treated
commends:	wishes
at large:	described in full
Glendower:	Henry, of course, does not yet know the Welsh army has disbanded: whether Shakespeare identified Glendower with the Welsh Captain of II.4 is not clear

Act III Scene 2

In this extraordinarily rich and justly famous scene we meet Richard for the first time since he left for Ireland in II.1. In the scenes which have followed since then the balance of power has shifted decisively to Henry who, without a struggle, has become effective ruler of all England. Now Richard is to learn what the audience already knows, the true state of things. As he does so, we learn three things about him: (*i*) that he is capable of poetic expression of haunting beauty; (*ii*) that he is emotionally unstable; and (*iii*) that he is far from being a skilled leader of men and is incapable of resolute action. Taken together, these features humanise Richard so that, the sordid tyrant of the earlier scenes now largely forgotten, we feel a new sympathy for him as we watch his sensitive nature struggle with adversity. The scene follows Richard as he see-saws between hope and despair.

Richard lands at Barkloughly, and is overjoyed to be back in his kingdom. He beseeches the earth itself to help him against the rebels (there is pathetic irony here in the fact that we know, as Richard does not, that *men* will not help him). The Bishop of Carlisle assures Richard that God can keep him King, but adds that men should exert themselves to bring about God's will. Aumerle more pointedly says that they must make plans to deal with Henry. Richard rejects this as advice unworthy of a king: he is idealistically (and impractically) confident in the power of his mere kingly presence to win support and shame Henry and his followers into submission (lines 1–62).

Then the first blow falls: Salisbury arrives with the news that the Welsh army has disbanded (as we saw in II.4). Immediately Richard is plunged into despair, but he revives upon recalling that he is still King and that this is worth 'twenty thousand' men (lines 62–90).

And then the second blow falls: Scroop comes and paints a dismal picture of an entire kingdom in arms against its king, to conclude with the news that Richard's favourites have been executed (as we saw in III.1). Richard's despair this time is deeper: in one of Shakespeare's most famous speeches (lines 144–77) he dwells on death and the futility of

kingly splendour. However, he revives again when Aumerle reminds him
that there is still his father York and his army (lines 91–191).

The third blow follows: unwillingly Scroop admits that York has
defected to Henry. Richard now refuses all comfort. As far as he is
concerned, the situation is hopeless. He discharges his soldiers and
abandons the contest without even a fight. His sun has set: it is now
'Bolingbroke's fair day' (lines 192–218).

This is the pivotal scene of the play: power has finally slipped from
Richard, even though his submission to Henry and deposition are yet to
come.

NOTES AND GLOSSARY:

Bishop of Carlisle: Thomas Merke (died 1409), one of Richard's
staunchest supporters
Barkloughly: the modern Harlech in Wales
Brooks: enjoys
salute: greet
fondly: lovingly and foolishly
And ... hands: that is, because Richard touches the earth with his
hands (line 6), and to be touched by a royal hand is a
privilege
sweets: good things harvested from the earth
venom: it was thought spiders sucked up poison from the
earth
heavy-gated: slow-footed, cumbersome
treacherous feet: that is, the rebels
double tongue: snakes have forked tongues
my ... conjuration: my solemn appeal to things without sense
falter: stagger under, stumble before
power: God
heaven would: while heaven would keep you King
And ... not: we would fail to keep you King (by failing to take
the necessary action)
searching eye: the sun: Richard compares his absence in Ireland to
the absence of the sun at night when it lights the
earth elsewhere
Behind ... world: the line is obscure: many editors change 'that' to
'and', which makes clear sense
terrestial ball: the earth
He: that is, the sun: Richard's suggestion in the following lines is that just as criminals who prefer to act
under cover of darkness (lines 39–40) flee when the
sun comes up, so his mere presence will frighten the
rebels into submission

with ... Antipodes:	with (the people who live on) the opposite side of the earth: Richard had, of course, only been to Ireland, but he continues the comparison of his absence to that of the sun
self-affrighted:	self-condemned
rude:	violent
balm:	oil with which a king is consecrated at his coronation
worldly:	earthly (as opposed to the heavenly power which makes a king)
The ... Lord:	the line refers to the belief, crucial to Richard's thinking, that a king is chosen for his sacred office by God and so is answerable only to him
pressed:	forced, conscripted
shrewd:	harmful, malicious
steel:	that is, swords
crown, angel:	both these were coins
still:	always
dead:	as if dead
All ... fly:	either 'all people who wish to be safe do fly' or 'let all people who wish to be safe fly'
blot:	stain (in that he has been deserted by the Welsh)
subject:	subject of the King, citizen
Scroop:	Sir Stephen Scroop (died 1408), one of the few who remained faithful to Richard even after his arrest (not the Earl of Wiltshire, see note on page 46)
betide:	may (more health and happiness) come to
care ... tongue:	tongue that must speak of sorrow
limits:	its proper bounds
Whitebeards:	old men
speak big:	that is, like men
clap:	force
female:	womanish, weak
arms:	armour
beadsmen:	men paid to pray for others
double fatal:	as the yew tree is poisonous and its wood was made for making bows it was a double cause of death
distaff women:	women who would usually spin thread
manage:	wield
bills:	weapons with long wooden handles and axes' heads
Bagot ... Green:	Bagot was not executed at Bristol, nor had Shakespeare included him amongst those killed in III.1 (although he had mistakenly placed him there in II.3.163–4), yet, before Richard knows this (lines

141–2) he exclaims against only *three* Judases in line 132 after having named *four* men here, and similarly at line 141 Aumerle, for no clear reason, names only three of the four: this looks like a simple slip on Shakespeare's part

Measure our confines: walk over our lands

peaceful: unopposed

prevail: are victorious

Judas: the disciple who betrayed Jesus (Luke 22:47–8)

Would: were they willing to

property: quality

heads ... hands: that is, not by shaking Henry's hand but by sacrificing their heads

graved: buried

executor: a man who carries out the instructions of a will

model: the mound raised over a grave

paste and cover: an image taken from a pie crust, since this was sometimes called a coffin

antic: jester: death was often pictured as a skeleton grinning at the preoccupations of men with power and wealth

Scoffing his state: mocking his (that is, the King's)

monarchize: play the King

kill with looks: that is, because a king could decree someone's death with a mere glance of displeasure

self: of himself (an adjective governing 'conceit')

humoured thus: that is, either death having been thus entertained for a while by this spectacle of men pretending to be powerful, or the King having been thus lulled for a while by enjoying his pomp

Cover ... heads: ordinarily men would uncover their heads before a monarch

For ... while: that is, both because Richard is not the mighty king he has seemed to be (death is the real ruler) and because he is a man like any other

But ... wail: but stop the cause of grief by prompt action

in: through, because of

Fear ... fight: if you are afraid, you will be killed, yet no worse can befall if you (are brave enough to) fight

And ... breath: to die fighting is to destroy death's power over you by refusing to be in awe of him, whereas to fear to die is to be the slave of death as long as you live

And ... limb: that is, learn to make what army he has serve for all the forces you should have

overblown:	passed
My tongue:	see that (or 'judge', line 194) my tongue
Beshrew:	a mild oath
ear:	plough
grow:	literally 'cultivate', but in terms of the image, 'prosper'

Act III Scene 3

It is now August 1399 and in this scene the confrontation between Henry and Richard we have been so long expecting comes about. However, it occurs in a curious way. In Holinshed, Northumberland meets Richard in Wales, persuades him to set out to meet Henry with a promise of safe conduct, and then has him ambushed and taken as a prisoner to Flint Castle where Henry comes to him. In other words, Henry contrives to have Richard captured. In this scene, however, Henry and his followers do not know that Richard is in Flint Castle, and they are most surprised when they find out (lines 20–30). The effect of this change on Shakespeare's part is once again to stress the ease with which Henry succeeds: he literally stumbles upon the King, having planned nothing. Fate is clearly on his side.

The scene opens on an ominous note: York chides Northumberland for neglecting to call Richard 'King Richard', and voices the first clear suspicion in the play that Henry is after more than his rights as Duke of Lancaster (lines 16–17). Nevertheless, when Henry discovers that Richard is in the castle, he sends Northumberland as his messenger to proclaim that that *is* all he wants, with the repeal of his banishment (lines 31–42). In a fine moment, Richard appears on the castle battlements (that is, on the balcony over the stage) and speaks with all the regal dignity and apparent confidence of which he is capable (lines 71–100). Northumberland's address (lines 101–20) explains Henry's demands and that Henry will submit and disband his army if they are granted. The words sound well, but Northumberland also stresses (as Henry had instructed, lines 42–4) Henry's military superiority and his willingness to fight to gain what he wants. In other words, Richard has no choice. This the King recognises: he immediately agrees to all Henry's terms (lines 121–6), though he is ashamed to do so (lines 127–30) and does not believe for a moment that Henry will be satisfied with what he has asked for. Richard is in no doubt that Henry aims at the crown, and is fully aware that he is in the power of 'King Bolingbroke', as he calls him (lines 142–75). He descends to meet Henry and agrees to go to London. Though the scene ends with Henry having said nothing about his plans, we have little doubt that Richard's interpretation of them is correct and that he will be deposed.

NOTES AND GLOSSARY:

So ... learn:	the scene begins in mid-conversation
intelligence:	information (presumably Henry is reading a letter)
Welshmen:	in III.1.43 Henry had been planning to fight the Welsh; he has now learned what we saw in II.4 and Richard was told in III.2.64–74, that the Welsh army has disbanded
beseem:	become, be fitting
mistakes:	is mistaken
Would ... been:	when, if you had been
to shorten:	as to shorten
For ... head:	both (*i*) for acting impetuously (in forgetting courtesy) and (*ii*) for depriving the King of his title
your ... length:	that is, by executing him
mistake the heavens:	misinterpret the will of God
castle:	namely, Flint Castle, as we soon learn (lines 21–5, and see III.2.209)
Noble lord:	Northumberland
rude ribs:	rough walls
brazen:	brass
breath of parley:	trumpet call to invite an opponent to negotiations
his:	that is, both Richard's and (metaphorically) the castle's
advantage ... power:	superiority of my forces
stooping duty:	kneeling
without ... drum:	that is, without warlike and threatening noise
tattered:	dilapidated
appointments:	equipment
Of fire ... heaven:	it was believed that thunder was caused by the meeting of the elements of fire (lightning) and water (rain)
Be ... water:	fire was the primary of the four elements (earth, air, fire, water), so Henry appears to be saying that he is willing for Richard to be the superior, that is, King
eagle:	the first among (king of) birds
watch:	watch for, wait for
fearful:	in fear, submissive
awful:	in awe, respectful
duty:	the kneeling required of a dutiful subject
profane:	commit sacrilege
torn ... souls:	sinned
pestilence:	plagues: Richard is probably recalling the plagues God sent against the Egyptians on behalf of Moses and the Israelites (Exodus 8:1–11:10)
unbegot:	not yet conceived

That:	of you who
testament ... war:	will which bequeaths bloody war
crowns:	heads
Shall ... face:	that is, lie on the ground
pastor's:	shepherd's, with a hint of the religious sense of pastor as priest
civil ... arms:	weapons used in civil war barbarously
one ... head:	namely, Edward III's
scope:	intention, aim
lineal royalties:	rights due through inheritance
Enfranchisement:	freedom from banishment
commend to rust:	commit to rust, lay aside
barbed:	armoured
poorly:	abjectly
lend:	supplies
sooth:	appeasement
scope:	room
scope:	permission
A:	in
beads:	a rosary, used by Roman Catholics to assist the memory in prayer
almsman:	man who lives on charity
figured:	ornamented
palmer:	pilgrim
carved saints:	carved wooden models of saints
trade:	traffic
buried once:	once buried
lodge:	beat down
pretty match:	game
fretted:	worn away
and ... lies:	the sense requires a break after 'laid': 'and therein are we laid; our epitaph might be "there lies ..."'
idly:	foolishly
Will ... die:	Richard already sees that his life is in danger when he asks this question, which must be answered 'yes' whatever Henry intends to do
make ... leg:	bend the knee, curtsey
base-court:	lower courtyard on ground level
Phaethon:	the son of the sun god Apollo, who, taking his father's chariot, was unable to control it and was killed by a thunderbolt from Zeus to prevent him from colliding with the earth
wanting the manage:	unable to control
jades:	contemptuous term for horses

base-court:	Richard plays on the other sense of 'base', despicable, ignoble
do ... grace:	submit to them
mounting:	climbing (the lark sings as it ascends)
fondly:	foolishly
frantic:	mad
apart:	back
Me ... had:	I had rather that
Thus:	Richard gestures to the crown on his head
redoubted:	dreaded, feared
want ... remedies:	but cannot remedy the cause of weeping

Act III Scene 4

The second of the three scenes (the others are the beginning of II.1 and V.1) in which Shakespeare, departing from his sources, concentrates upon the Queen (whom he makes a mature woman to gain his effect) in an attempt to win our sympathy for Richard. From II.2.116–7, III.1.36 and line 70 we may gather that the scene is set in the Duke of York's garden, but an audience could hardly be expected to work this out: that it is a garden (line 1), far from the events of III.2–3, and after Richard has set out for London, is what is important.

The Queen, ignorant of what has become of Richard, wishes she might be entertained to take her mind off her worries, but she cannot be satisfied with any of her ladies' suggestions. When the gardeners enter, she retires to overhear their conversation. As she expected, they talk of public affairs. In their conversation Shakespeare develops in detail the comparison of the state of England under Richard to an unweeded and untended garden. This analogy has been used before in the play, and was a common one with writers, especially satirists and commentators on state events, of Shakespeare's time. It reminds us here that Richard himself, by his negligence, is ultimately responsible for his downfall. The news that Richard is now in Henry's power wrings from the Queen a cry of disbelief. The scene ends as she resolves to travel to London herself.

NOTES AND GLOSSARY:

sport:	pastime
rubs:	difficulty (a technical term in bowls for something which obstructs the 'wood' or bowl)
bias:	a wood is weighted on one side (the 'bias') so that it rolls in a curve: to run 'against the bias' is thus to go in a direction other than the one the wood would naturally take, and so the Queen means her fortune is going against her wishes, that is, badly

keep no measure:	'follow the steps of a dance' and 'keep time'
measure:	limit
altogether had:	possessed completely
it boots ... complain:	there is no point in lamenting
shouldst:	would
And I ... thee:	and if my troubles were only such as weeping could make better then I would sing for joy and have no need to ask you to weep for me
My ... pins:	I will bet my sadness against a row of pins (that is, something very great against something very small, implying she is confident they will 'talk of state')
Against a change:	when they expect a change
Woe ... woe:	that is, sad events are preceded by men foreseeing and lamenting them
apricocks:	apricots
Stop ... weight:	prodigal means both 'excessive' and 'wastefully extravagant', so the line suggests a father literally bowed down with the weight of his children and metaphorically bowed down with the cares their extravagance causes him
sprays:	clumps of buds or flowers on one stem
even:	equal
in:	under
You:	while you are
noisome:	harmful
within ... pale:	within the limits of a fence
proportion:	order
as ... model:	that is, perfectly
firm estate:	stable administration of government
sea ... garden:	that is, England (the sea being the 'wall' or 'moat defensive' of Gaunt's speech, II.1.46—9)
knots:	flower-beds
caterpillars:	the word Henry used of Richard's favourites in II.3.165
suffered:	allowed, tolerated
fall of leaf:	autumn
trimmed:	pruned
at ... year:	at the appropriate time of year
overproud:	too luxuriant
confound:	destroy
bearing boughs:	boughs which bear fruit
O ... speaking:	the Queen uses a legal metaphor: a person charged with a crime who refused to plead either 'guilty' or 'not guilty' (that is, who remained silent, as the

Queen has done while listening to this conversation) was 'pressed' with weights until either he spoke and made a plea or died (a man might prefer so to die if he were liable to be found guilty, since, not having been proved guilty at his death, his heir could still inherit his possessions)

old Adam: Adam was a gardener in Eden (Genesis 2:15); he is called 'old' to distinguish him from the 'new Adam', Christ

serpent: the serpent tempted Eve to eat the forbidden fruit in Eden and so caused the fall of man from happiness (Genesis 3:1–24)

suggested: tempted

weighed: balanced against each other

scale: tray of a pair of weighing scales

vanities: follies, and, especially, Richard's favourites

embassage: message

serve me: deliver your message to me

What: in this instance, an exclamation, rather than a question

so ... worse: that is, if it would prevent your situation from worsening

rue: herb

ruth: pity

Act IV Scene 1

A Shakespearean play commonly moves to a climax at the end of the third act or beginning of the fourth, and then the tension relaxes before the final climax. It is now autumn 1399 and what Henry has achieved is about to be given formal recognition. The scene thus marks the climax of the action which has given Henry more and more power and Richard less and less. The scene occupies the whole act, and is made up of the following incidents.

(1) The scene opens with Henry asking Bagot for details of the circumstances of Gloucester's death. His enquiries lead to a series of challenges and counter-challenges as the noblemen present argue fiercely about whether Aumerle was or was not responsible for Gloucester's murder. Who actually accuses whom of what here is less important than the impression of violent disorder which is built up dangerously close to comic proportions (Aumerle, for example, runs out of gages with which to challenge people!). It is not a very dignified sight. We remember the play began with Richard sitting in judgement on a quarrel about Gloucester's death; that had been a formal and splendid occasion. As

Henry is about to begin his reign, he too sits in judgement on a similar quarrel, but this is an unruly, almost ridiculous, squabble. The audience must feel that his reign—his 'new world' (line 78)—is going to be less grand, less splendid, than Richard's. Thus, Shakespeare begins the scene by impressing on us that, whatever Richard's failings, something fine is lost when he ceases to be king (lines 1–106).

(2) York then enters to say that Richard will willingly give up the crown, and he hails Henry as King Henry IV. At this the Bishop of Carlisle protests and, in a speech crucial to the political ideas of the play, he argues that no subject can possibly judge, let alone depose, an anointed king, and that if the noblemen present recognise Henry as king then, the crown having been taken away from the true king, rivalries among the descendants of Edward III for the throne will result in civil war for years to come. Thus, just before we see Richard, Shakespeare reminds us of the arguments on his side and of the enormity and terrible consequences of what is about to happen. We begin to see that Shakespeare is carefully arranging the scene to win maximum sympathy for Richard. However, the Bishop is arrested for his trouble: though we may sympathise with Richard, we see that nothing is going to prevent Henry carrying through his plan (lines 107–61).

(3) There follows the deposition scene. Henry has planned that Richard should publicly announce his willingness to give up the throne and read a list of those crimes he has committed which make him unfit to rule. Richard does abdicate, but cannot bring himself to read out the list, and Henry tells Northumberland to stop trying to make him do so. Two things are significant in this scene. First of all, although it is Henry who has arranged the affair, he says very little, and it is Richard who is the centre of attention. Secondly, Richard is in a confused state of mind, worn out by sadness, oppressed by the hopelessness of his situation and (as he believes) the injustice of what is happening. He cannot believe he is not the King, and yet recognises he cannot continue to rule. The spectacle of a man thus reduced to nothing is deeply moving (lines 162–319).

(4) Finally, we hear, in the conversation between the Abbot of Westminster, the Bishop of Carlisle and Aumerle, of a plot to overthrow Henry and restore Richard. No sooner is Henry on the throne than troubles follow. It seems the Bishop of Carlisle's prophecy is already coming true. In showing us so soon that Henry's reign will not be easy, Shakespeare again prevents us from siding with him, as he has done throughout this scene (lines 320–33).

In order to prepare us to view Richard's abdication, the centre of the scene, sympathetically, and to show discontent following immediately, Shakespeare has here both altered the sequence of events and speeded them up. In Holinshed, the order is as follows: the paragraph numbers used in the above summary of the scene show what Shakespeare has done.

(3)	29 September 1399	Richard abdicates
(2)	30 September 1399	Henry takes the throne
(1)	16 October 1399	Bagot accuses Aumerle
(2)	22 October 1399	Carlisle's defence of Richard
(1)	27 October 1399	Henry decides to send for Mowbray
(4)	December 1399	the Abbot's plot

NOTES AND GLOSSARY:

Fitzwater: Walter Baron Fitzwalter (1368–1406?), a supporter of Henry

Surrey: Sir Thomas Howard (1374–1400), Duke of Surrey and Earl of Kent, finally executed for his staunch opposition to Henry (see V.6.8, where he is referred to as 'Kent'): it seems Shakespeare did not identify him with the Lord Marshal in I.1 and I.3 (see notes on pages 24 and 37)

Abbot of Westminster: William of Colchester

Bagot: it seems Shakespeare assumes he has deserted Richard's cause and is now co-operating with Henry, although he had (and in history did) planned to go to Ireland (II.2.140)

who ... end: that is, who actually killed him (in addition to those who were in the plot)

timeless: 'untimely

of ... reacheth: so long that it can reach

Calais: a port in northern France where Gloucester was murdered

uncle: Gloucester

In that ... death: the chronology is incorrect here: Gloucester was killed at Calais in 1397, long before Henry was banished in the autumn of 1398, so Aumerle could not have remarked at the time of Gloucester's death (lines 10, 14) that he would rather Henry never returned from banishment

Than ... return: than that Bolingbroke should return

fair stars: noble birth (since this was due to the kind of influence of the stars at the time)

equal terms: a knight was not bound to fight with his social inferior, and compared to Aumerle (grandson of Edward III), Bagot is 'base'

attainder: accusation

manual ... death:	a legal document receives its authority from the seal placed on it to prove it is valid: Aumerle's gesture with his hand ('manual') is the proof (or 'seal') that he will kill his accuser
temper:	quality, and, more specifically, brightness of a sword blade
Excepting ... so:	I wish the man who has so angered ('moved') me was the best knight in this company ('presence') with the exception of one (namely, Henry)
stand:	insists
sympathy:	equal rank
rapier:	light Italian sword with a point but no blade; it was coming into fashion in England in Shakespeare's time but was quite unknown in the fourteenth century
to the ... breathing:	to the death
I ... like:	I lay on the earth a similar task (namely, to support my gage)
hollowed:	shouted, hollered
sun to sun:	sunrise to sunset (the prescribed limits for a combat)
Engage ... trial:	accept the challenge
Who ... else?	who else challenge me?
boy:	a term of contempt here
That lie:	namely, that Fitzwater's charge in line 65 that Surrey lied when he said in line 64 that it was a lie Aumerle boasted of killing Gloucester (lines 35–7)
fondly:	needlessly
forward:	willing (that is, line 71 is needless as Fitzwater is only too ready to accept)
There ... faith:	his gage (either another thrown down, or pointing to the one thrown down to challenge Aumerle at line 34)
correction:	punishment
new world:	that is, the new order of things established by Henry
Norfolk:	Mowbray (see notes on pages 24 and 26)
Some ... gage:	Aumerle has already used one on Bagot (line 24) and one at line 57
rest ... gage:	remain as challenges (and not come to trial yet)
Streaming ... cross:	a red cross was the badge of the Crusaders (see line 100), which Carlisle imagines blowing ('streaming') on a flag ('ensign') as Mowbray charges the enemy
pagans:	actually, of course, Muslims
Saracen:	Arab
toiled:	exhausted

bosom ... Abraham: heaven (Luke 16:22)

plume-plucked: humbled

Worst ... truth: though, as a bishop, I may be the least important person ('worst' meaning lowest rank) to speak in this royal company, yet it best becomes me (rather than anyone else) to speak the truth

noblesse: nobility

Learn ... wrong: teach him to refrain from so foul a wrong (as sitting in judgement on a king)

by: present

refined: purified (by their Christian faith)

kind: fellow countrymen

mutiny: discord, strife

Golgotha: Hebrew name for the hill where Christ was crucified, translated as 'a place of a skull' in the King James Bible (1611), but as 'a place of dead men's skulls' in the earlier Bible translation available at the time of the play (Matthew 27:33)

this ... house: the family (or 'house') of Plantagenet, which was indeed to divide into the rival houses of York (descendants of the Duke of York) and Lancaster (descendants of Gaunt)

child ... children: that is, three generations hence

Of ... treason: on a charge of treason punishable by death

commons' suit: the request of the House of Commons (which had asked that the reasons for Richard's loss of his throne should be publicly stated)

conduct: conductor

you ... arrest: that is, the appellants (line 104) of the first part of the scene

Procure ... sureties: produce your guarantees that you will appear on the day appointed (the surety would probably take the form of a lord willing to swear he would ensure that the appellant comes)

looked for expected (the way you have behaved)

clerk assistant at a Christian service who would make the response 'Amen' to the priest's prayers

tired majesty: the pretence arranged by Henry is that Richard freely gives up his throne because its responsibilities have worn him out

owes: owns, is equipped with

Your care ... they stay: the sense of 'care' changes throughout this teasing passage: 'Your taking on of responsibility ('Your cares') does not take away my troubles ('my cares'). My cause of grief ('My care') is that I have lost the responsibility of kingship ('loss of care') through the follies ('old care') I committed ('done'). Your source of worry ('Your care') is that you have gained responsibility ('gain of care') through the care with which you have carried out your recent plans ('by new care won'). Although I have given you the worries of office ('The cares I give') I have troubles still ('I have'), though apparently given to you, since I cannot give away the crown without guilt, regret and shame. Anxiety and sorrow may attend the crown ('tend the crown'), yet they remain with me though I am no longer the king'.

Ay ... be: 'Ay' (yes) and 'I' sound alike, and so the puns suggest both Richard's indecision ('yes, no, no, yes') and his despair ('I am nothing, no "I" exists'), as well as the torment of a mind now powerless to do anything but play with words

Therefore ... thee: as you can see, I am not contented, but I do resign in your favour

undo: both 'undress' (as he removes the symbols of kingship) and 'ruin'

with ... grieved: both 'grieved with having nothing' and 'grieved by nothing'

earthly pit: grave

read: Northumberland offers Richard a document listing his crimes

ravel out: reveal

weaved up: continues the image of 'ravel out' (literally, to pull out a thread from a piece of cloth or ball of thread): the meaning is that Richard will have to state each single detail (or thread) of all the foolish actions (the cloth) of his life

article: item

cracking ... oath: breaking the firm and solemn undertaking of your oath of allegiance (to Richard)

Pilate: Pontius Pilate, unable to discover clear proof of guilt in Christ, washed his hands when he condemned him to show he was not responsible for his death (Matthew 27:24)

sour cross: bitter suffering (Christ was crucified on a cross)

sort: gang (a contemptuous word)

pompous: covered with pomp, splendid

state: grandeur, royal rank

heavy:	sad
sterling:	valid, can command
hither straight:	be brought here immediately
wink:	close their eyes to
faced:	allowed, countenanced
outfaced:	overcome
shadow:	(line 291) consequence of your sorrow (that is, breaking the glass); (line 292) merely the image
'Tis very true:	Henry's dismissive lines (lines 291–2) had tried to stop Richard's performance by pointing out he had broken only a mirror and not, as he claimed (line 290), been destroyed by sorrow; Richard takes up the word 'shadow' to agree with Henry, but, in the following lines, argues that his actions are the consequences (or shadows) of a *real* grief, just as the mirror reflected a real face
to:	(line 296) of; (line 307) to be
from ... sights:	out of the sight of all of you
Conveyors:	a pun on 'convey' in the sense of 'steal'
pageant:	spectacle
take ... intents:	swear on the sacrament (the consecrated bread given in the Holy Communion service which Christians believe to be the body of Christ) not only to conceal my plans
effect:	carry out

Act V Scene 1

The last of the three scenes invented by Shakespeare to win sympathy for Richard through his Queen (see also II.2 and III.4). The Queen (who has come to London to seek out Richard, III.4.96–7) meets Richard on his way to the Tower (where he was despatched by Henry, IV.1.315). She is dismayed at the change in him and, especially, at his loss of will to fight back at his enemies. Northumberland interrupts them to say that Richard is now to go to Pomfret in Yorkshire, and not the Tower, and that the Queen must leave for France. Richard foretells that Northumberland and Henry will fall out before long, but Northumberland is not impressed and hurries to part the two. They take their last farewell in great sadness. In IV.1 we saw the political tragedy of Richard: here we see the human tragedy.

NOTES AND GLOSSARY:

Julius ... Tower:	the Tower of London, wrongly supposed to have been first built by Julius Caesar

ill-erected:	built for bad purposes (both because of the sufferings of those imprisoned within it and because it is to hold Richard from her)
flint:	flinty, stone and so (metaphorically) cold, unfeeling
soft:	wait
My ... rose:	Richard
model ... stand:	the Queen likens Richard in his fallen state to the ruins of the great city Troy after it had been sacked by the Greeks
old Troy:	tradition had it that London was founded by refugees from Troy who named it 'New Troy'
map:	form, image
King ... tomb:	because Richard the King is (metaphorically) dead, and this man has only the body or form of the King
inn, alehouse:	Richard is the 'beauteous inn' filled with grief, Henry the 'alehouse' where triumph is entertained
To . . . sudden:	to hasten my death
league:	alliance, contract
religious house:	nunnery, convent
new ... crown:	that is, a crown of righteousness in heaven
Which ... down:	either 'since our wicked lives here have lost us our earthly crown' or 'which crown of righteousness our wicked lives here have thrown away'
To be:	because he is
If ... beasts:	if of anything other than beasts (implying that only because his noblemen have behaved like animals is he no longer a king of men)
betid:	past
quite:	requite, answer
griefs:	tragic tales
For why:	because (of the tale's sadness)
brands:	logs burning on the fire
heavy accent:	sad sound
Pomfret:	Pontefract in Yorkshire
order ... you:	arrangements have been made for you
wherewithal:	whereby
Thou ... corruption:	in *2 Henry IV*, III.1.60–79, Henry quotes these lines when their prophecy has been fulfilled
head:	head of pus on a boil
helping:	since you have helped
one or both:	that is, either the King or the man who helped him to the throne, or both
kiss:	bride and groom complete the marriage ceremony with a kiss

pines the clime:	consumes or wears away the land
Hallowmas:	All Saints Day, now 1 November, but in Shakespeare's time 12 November and so near the shortest day, 22 December
That ... policy:	the quartos give this line to Richard, the Folio to Northumberland, whose down-to-earth common sense it seems to suit better
little policy:	bad politics
Better ... near:	it is better to be far apart than, being close together, to be no nearer seeing each other
So ... moans:	as the Queen is going all the way to France she will have most moaning to do if line 89 is carried out literally
piece:	lengthen
Thus ... heart:	it is a commonplace of Elizabethan love poetry that lovers exchange hearts with a kiss
mine own:	my own heart
To take ... heart:	to undertake to look after your heart and then kill it (when I die of grief)
We ... wanton:	we play with grief

Act V Scene 2

The Duke of York is telling his wife of the way in which Henry brought Richard to London (which had happened between III.3 and IV.1). The account serves, yet again, to win sympathy for Richard as York tells of his dignified bearing under the crowd's insults. When York's son, Aumerle, comes in, York insists on reading a paper he sees he is carrying, and from it learns that Aumerle is involved in the Abbot of Westminster's plot (IV.1.325–9). As York has taken an oath of allegiance to Henry, and has personally guaranteed the loyalty of his son, he is furious at this discovery and determined, despite his wife's pleas, to ride immediately to reveal the plot to the King. (This actually happened in January 1400, but it appears, from York's recounting of the arrival in London, to be only shortly after that happened in September 1399). The Duchess sends Aumerle to reach Henry before York and herself sets out immediately to follow.

NOTES AND GLOSSARY:

Duchess:	at this time actually York's second wife, Aumerle's mother, Isabella of Castile, having died in 1394, but Shakespeare makes the Duchess behave and speak (see line 103) as though she is Aumerle's mother, not his step-mother

two cousins:	that is, Henry and Richard
rude:	brutal, violent
misgoverned:	committing wrong
windows' tops:	windows of the upper storeys of buildings
hot and fiery:	eager and high spirited
seemed to know:	the horse is the subject of the verb (seemed to understand his ambitious rider)
course:	way
casements:	windows
and that:	and you would have thought that
painted imagery:	the walls of Elizabethan houses were often hung with tapestries and painted cloths depicting people with words coming out of their mouths
well graced:	elegant and well-received
idly:	without much interest
Thinking:	expecting
perforce:	inevitably, have been forced to
bound ... contents:	we must submit ourselves to calm content
for aye:	for ever, completely
But ... friend:	Aumerle was deprived of his dukedom for his part in the quarrel depicted at the beginning of IV.1
pledge ... truth:	guarantee his loyalty
fealty:	faithfulness
Who ... spring?:	that is, who are the new favourites at court?
had as lief:	would as willingly
justs and triumphs:	jousts or tournaments, and processions
seal:	the mark in red wax which signed a letter would hang down from it on a narrow strip of parchment and so could be outside Aumerle's clothes while the letter itself was in an inner pocket
consequence:	importance
bond:	agreement to pay back borrowed money
'gainst:	in preparation for
Bound ... to?:	York says that if the Duchess's suggestion is correct, the man who lent the money would have the document promising repayment: what, then, is Aumerle doing with it?
Poor ... amazed:	the Duchess supposes Aumerle is stunned by what is happening as he does not strike the servant
villain:	man (used to a servant without suggestion of criminality)
own:	own family
Have ... sons:	historically, York had another son, Richard, Earl of Cambridge, who appears in *Henry V*

teeming-date:	years of child-bearing
A dozen ... Oxford:	as the Abbot of Westminster had planned, IV.1.325–9
interchangeably ... hands:	that is, each conspirator has a document signed by all, so each has a record of the others' oaths
what ... him?:	what has what they do got to do with him?

Act V Scene 3

The first twenty-two lines of the scene show Henry concerned about the dissolute and irresponsible behaviour of his son, who frequents taverns and mocks the ideals of noble society. We do not meet him in this play, but he is to figure largely as Prince Hal in the *Henry IV* plays and to become the ideal king in *Henry V*. Henry's speech introduces what is to be the main theme of *1 Henry IV*: Hal's apparent unsuitableness to inherit the throne. The speech may thus indicate that Shakespeare already had that play in mind when he composed *Richard II* (see p. 14), but, here, its purpose is to add to the quarrelling nobles of IV.1, and the conspiracy about which Henry is to learn in a moment, another worry: the character of his son. It seems that, now he has gained the throne, Henry is indeed beset with those 'cares' described by Richard in IV.1.194–8.

Aumerle then enters, and the action follows directly on V.2. He begs Henry's pardon, which is granted, but before Henry can learn what it is that Aumerle planned to do, York arrives and reveals the plot. He argues strongly that Aumerle should not be pardoned, but then the Duchess arrives and she argues, just as strongly, that he should be. Henry finally confirms the pardon he has granted, but arranges for the other conspirators to be captured and put to death.

Something nearly comic had appeared at the beginning of IV.1 with the repeated challenges of the nobles. This lessened our respect for the new King's reign and was a marked contrast to the deposition which followed. After the sombre mood of V.1, relief came again in the near comedy of York struggling to put on his boots while the Duchess tried to prevent him. The same mood prevails here, with the succession of people banging on the door and the husband and wife contradicting each other so vehemently. Henry himself recognises that this is near to farce (lines 78–9). The scene does give a lighter mood before we come to the death of Richard, but we may well feel it is nevertheless rather out of place. After all, serious questions of loyalty to king and kin are at stake.

NOTES AND GLOSSARY:

plague:	cause of discontent, calamity

frequent:	goes regularly
watch:	night watchmen
passengers:	travellers
effeminate:	self-indulgent
Takes ... point:	takes it to be a point
gallant:	fine young man (contemptuous)
stews:	brothels
commonest creature:	meanest prostitute
favour:	knights at tournaments would wear some token ('favour') given them by a lady
lustiest:	most vigorous
desperate:	reckless
To ... conference:	that I may speak
Unless a:	unless I receive a
after-love:	future loyalty
make thee safe:	harmless (by killing him)
secure foolhardy:	over-confident and rash
Shall ... face?:	must I, because of my love and loyalty, speak treason (by calling you foolhardy) to your face?
my ... show:	my haste prevents me from explaining (because he is so short of breath)
confederate:	in accord with
Forget:	forget your promise
sheer:	pure
digressing:	wayward
bawd:	literally, a woman who procures prostitutes for men, and so, metaphorically, an encourager to vice
Or ... lies:	or my life lies shamed in his dishonour
A beggar ... before:	that is, I who never before begged for anything, beg you to grant this request
The Beggar ... king:	a reference to the ballad of King Cophetua who fell in love with a beggar maid: Henry means that the situation is becoming absurd, farcical, like the subject of the ballad
for:	on behalf of
This ... confound:	if you cut off this poisoned limb (Aumerle) the rest of the body (the court) will remain healthy, but if you leave it alone it will infect and destroy all the rest
itself:	that is, its own children
none other can:	cannot love another (and so not you, the King)
dugs:	breasts
rear:	raise up (by getting Aumerle pardoned and so raised to life)
Not yet ... boy:	so she had vowed to do, V.2.117–8

the happy sees:	those who are happy see
bid me joy:	invite me to have joy
grace:	favour (that is, grant a pardon)
breast:	heart
mercy:	kind response, charitable hearing
but not ... sweet:	but it is sweeter than it is short
'Pardonne-moi':	(*French*) *pardonnez-moi*, a polite way of refusing a request ('pardon me, but...')
Dost ... destroy?:	a reference to York's use of the word in the previous line: he teaches the King how to refuse to give a pardon by actually using the word 'pardon'
current:	valid (that is, with its English meaning)
chopping French:	French which changes the meaning of words
Set ... there:	let your tongue express (the pity I see in your eye)
Or in ... ear:	that is, so that he can hear how his heart responds to their plea
twain:	weaken by splitting it in two
brother-in-law:	John Holland, Duke of Exeter (1352?–1400), who married Henry's sister Elizabeth: he lost his dukedom at the same time as Aumerle and is mentioned at II.1.281, but has no part in the play
Abbot:	the Abbot of Westminster, who began the plot (IV.1.320–33)
consorted crew:	gang of associates
dog:	follow
order ... powers:	send several forces
I ... new:	a proverbial saying (deriving from the claim in 2 Corinthians 5:17 that any man in Christ is a 'new creature') meaning, in effect, 'let's make a new start'

Act V Scene 4

This short scene is based upon Holinshed's explanation of how Richard's death came about. In it, Sir Piers of Exton, a courtier who has overheard Henry say that he wished Richard were no longer alive to pose a threat to him, resolves to perform what he takes to be the will of the King, namely, the murder of Richard. Richard would be a source of anxiety to Henry because, as long as he lived, men might still be loyal to him and seek to restore him to the throne despite his supposedly willing abdication. Hence, Henry could only feel safe once Richard is dead.

NOTES AND GLOSSARY:

Sir Piers:	nothing is known of him, except that he was said to have murdered Richard

mark:	notice
will:	who will
wishtly:	longingly, intently
divorce:	separate, take away
rid:	rid him of

Act V Scene 5

This scene completes the process, begun in II.2 immediately after Richard left for Ireland, whereby our sympathy is won to Richard (see the scene summaries of II.2, III.2, IV.1, V.1). It is 14 February 1400. Richard is alone in prison at Pomfret (V.1.52). An air of foreboding and tension hangs over the opening of the scene as we know of Sir Piers's decision and know that murder is imminent. In one of Shakespeare's longest and finest soliloquies, Richard analyses his condition by comparing his thoughts and prison to people and the world, his life to music out of tune, and his prolonged sadness to the hours of a clock. We find that, stripped of all his pomp, he does now recognise that his loss of power is his own fault (lines 45–9). A humble groom enters: his loyalty and affection for the doomed Richard prepare for the final climax by bringing pathos to the scene. When his keeper refuses to taste his food, Richard realises that his last moment has come. If our sympathy had been won by his soliloquy, now our admiration is aroused as Richard fights bravely with his murderers. Shakespeare shows that Richard is, after all, a man of courage. But it is hopeless: the scene ends with Sir Piers regretting the murder the moment it is committed.

NOTES AND GLOSSARY:

And for because:	but since
populous:	populated, full of people
prove:	show to be, make
generation:	offspring, children
still-breeding:	thoughts which themselves multiply
this ... world:	that is, his prison (see line 21)
humours:	various temperaments, types
this world:	that is, the real world outside the prison
For:	that is, the thoughts that populate the world of his prison are like real people (line 10) because...
scruples:	doubts
set ... word:	that is, when a man thinks of God (line 12), he finds himself confused by apparent contradictions in the Bible (the Word of God)
Come ... eye:	these two texts come close together in Matthew 19:14, 24, Mark 10:14, 25, and Luke 18:16, 25: they

	are apparently contradictory in that the first seems to invite all to follow Christ while the second implies it is extremely difficult, if not impossible, to do so
'It is ... eye':	Biblical scholars then and now dispute the meaning of these words: the sense may be either that it is difficult for a camel to pass through a small gate in a city wall ('needle'), or for a rope ('camel') to pass through a needle's eye: 'postern' (small door) suggests the former, but 'thread' the latter, so it seems Shakespeare was well aware of the difficulty and chose his words deliberately to heighten the ambiguity so as to give weight to Richard's point that 'thoughts of things divine' are troubled by 'scruple' (lines 12–13)
Thoughts ... ambition:	Richard continues to illustrate his point at lines 10–11 by turning, after 'divine thoughts' (line 12), to worldly thoughts of ambition
nails:	finger nails
flinty ribs:	stone walls
ragged:	rough
And ... cannot:	and because they cannot (that is, ambitious thoughts cannot achieve this wonder, line 19–20)
Thoughts ... content:	a third illustration of lines 10–11
seely:	simple-minded
stocks:	a timber frame with holes for feet and sometimes hands, set in a public place, in which people were locked in a sitting position for minor offences
refuge ... shame:	seek refuge from their shame (that is, comfort themselves in their disgrace)
That many have:	with the thought that many others have sat
Thus ... people:	that is, by entertaining these different kinds of thoughts (lines 11, 18, 23) which are the people of his world (lines 6–10): Richard now goes on to show how, in his mind, he can assume different roles
am I:	I fancy myself, think that I am
crushing penury:	crippling poverty
that ... is:	that is only a man
With ... pleased:	will not be pleased with anything
being nothing:	that is, dead (the conclusion to the thought Richard introduced at line 11, that we are never content in our minds)
Ha, ha:	an exclamation (not a laugh) as he hears the musician make a mistake
time:	rhythm

no … kept:	the melody and notes are not properly played
music … lives:	Richard now compares a well-ordered life to a well-played piece of music
daintiness:	fineness, niceness
check:	rebuke
string:	stringed instrument
concord:	harmony
my:	my own (emphatic: Richard can hear when another plays badly but did not notice when he ruled badly)
state:	kingdom
time:	life
time:	rhythm (the 'music' of his life)
numbering clock:	clock which tells the hours
thoughts are minutes:	Richard moves on to a third image (after 'world' and 'music')
My thoughts … tears:	in these complex lines Richard expresses the hopelessness and futility of his position by seeing himself as having nothing to do but mark the passing of time with his grief: we might paraphrase as follows: 'Since I now have nothing to do but watch time pass, my thoughts are like minutes, only ways of measuring time. And, as my thoughts are sad ones, so the sighs they cause mark out the passage of time ('Their watches') like the ticks ('jars') made by the pendulum of a clock. But instead of looking on the dial of a clock to tell the time, time for me is registered in the tears in my eyes ('unto my eyes'), which thus become themselves like the outer edge of a clock face ('outward watch') to which my finger points, like a clock hand ('dial's point') as it wipes away my tears'
my time:	that is, the time which should have been Richard II's
jack:	a small figure of a man which on some clocks strikes the hours and quarters
mads:	maddens
holp:	helped (music was thought to cure madness: see, for example, *King Lear*, IV.7)
strange brooch:	rare jewel
royal, noble, groats:	puns on coins: a royal (50p), a noble (33p), a groat (1½p): the difference between a royal and a noble was thus ten groats (so Richard means that in calling him 'royal' the groom has valued him too highly as he is now merely the equal ('peer') of the groom)
dog:	fellow, man (contemptuous)

earned:	grieved
roan:	mixed colour
Barbary:	a breed of horse, but also here the name of Richard's own horse
dressed:	groomed
he:	Barbary
clapping:	patting
Forgiveness:	I ask your forgiveness
galled:	made sore
jauncing:	the movement of a rider in the saddle
Here ... stay:	you may stay here no longer
fall to:	begin (eating)
Taste ... do:	that is, to ensure it is not poisoned
What ... assault?:	either 'do you mean to kill me with this vicious attack?' or 'what does death mean by coming on me so suddenly in this vicious attack?'

Act V Scene 6

In this scene we learn first that the rebels have been defeated and executed, with the exception of the Bishop of Carlisle, whom Henry allows to live in a monastery. Piers then brings in the body of Richard. Henry, though he admits Richard's death is convenient for him, is appalled at the murder and refuses Piers thanks or reward. The play ends not in triumph and rejoicing, even though Henry now has the crown, the rebels are defeated and Richard is dead, but in sadness and guilt: Henry, 'full of woe/That blood should sprinkle me to make me grow', proposes a crusade to make amends for what has been done in his name. It is now March 1400, not quite two years since Henry charged Mowbray with treason.

NOTES AND GLOSSARY:

rebels:	the 'dozen' mentioned by York in V.2.97, who, when the plot to kill Henry was discovered (V.2–3), rose in open rebellion
Ciceter:	Cirencester
The heads:	the heads of traitors were stuck on poles on London Bridge
Salisbury ... Kent:	For Salisbury see note on beginning of II.4: Spencer is Thomas Le Despenser (1373–1400), Earl of Gloucester, who lost his earldom at the same time as Aumerle (see note on V.2.41–3); Blunt is Sir Thomas Blount; for Kent see note on Surrey at the beginning of IV.1

Fitzwater:	see note on beginning of IV.1
Brocas ... Seely:	Sir Leonard Brokas and Sir Bennet Seely, supporters of Richard
clog:	burden
of his pride:	for what his pride led him to do
secret:	retired, sheltered
reverent room:	religious retreat (monastery)
More ... hast:	that is, a situation more withdrawn and religious than you have occupied in the past
for thou ... land:	what you have done with your deadly hand has brought disgrace and shame on me and to this famous land
Cain:	after he murdered his brother Abel, Cain was condemned to wander the earth as an outcast (Genesis 4:10–16)
incontinent:	immediately
voyage ... Land:	that is, undertake a crusade to Jerusalem as a form of penance
Grace:	honour

Part 3

Commentary

Plot and structure

Richard II has a simple plot. The main sequence of events is easy to follow and, save for the York family business in V.2–3, our attention is never diverted from Richard and Henry and their interlocking fortunes. The action proceeds in four clear stages:

Richard as king: I.1–II.1
The rise of Henry: II.2–III.1
The transference of power: III.2–IV.1
Henry as king: V.1–4

Put like this, we can see how simple the plot is: as king, Richard banishes Henry; Henry returns; Richard yields to him; Henry is king. The pivotal point, the turning point of this action, is III.2, in which Richard, having returned from Ireland, abandons all hope of defeating Henry. In effect, he capitulates then: from this moment there can be no doubt of the outcome.

That scene, III.2, can, however, alert us to some of the peculiarities of the plot of this play. Richard has yet to meet Henry, but, from his high hopes and optimism at the beginning of the scene, he comes by the end of the scene to such black despair that he discharges his followers. He has given up. Henry has won, and there has been no fight. There are other examples of things happening without any struggle. II.3 opens with Henry crossing Gloucestershire with his army, but it seems to be more like a sight-seeing tour, or a triumphal progress, than an invasion. There is no opposition at all, and, at the end of the scene, York, who has boasted that the power of the King lies on him (II.3.95–7), simply admits that he cannot stop Henry and invites him to spend the night with him in Berkeley Castle. Or again, in III.1, Henry has apparently captured Bushy and Green with the greatest of ease, and he simply has them executed.

The point is that, most unusually for a history play, this is a play in which nothing physically happens. In I.3 we have all the ceremony and pomp of a tournament but, just as the combat is about to begin, it is stopped. There is an army of Welshmen who, instead of fighting, simply fade away (II.4). There is a kind of struggle between a monarch and a

usurper, but it is a very peculiar kind of struggle. Henry foresees his
meeting with Richard like this:

> Methinks King Richard and myself should meet
> With no less terror than the elements
> Of fire and water when their thundering shock
> At meeting tears the cloudy cheeks of heaven.
>
> (III.3.54–7)

But there is no such great and elemental conflict as these lines suggest.
On the contrary, Richard and Henry meet with no shock at all at Flint
Castle: they exchange very formal speeches—they merely talk, that is—
and then Richard submits and the contest is over.

The great scenes of the play, then, are not scenes of action: no actual
fighting occurs in the play until Richard's murder in V.5. The scenes to
which Shakespeare devoted most attention are static scenes, either of
formal dignity (such as I.1 and I.3), or of emotional stress (III.2, V.1, the
beginning of V.5), or both (III.3, IV.1). They are all scenes in which
people talk but do not act. In this play Shakespeare has chosen to devote
most space to those moments when people confront each other and
strive to have their way by the force of their words—Henry and
Mowbray (I.1), Gaunt and Richard (II.1), York and Henry (II.3),
Henry and Richard (III.3). This stress on people arguing with each other
comes to a climax in the spectacle of York and the Duchess of York each
striving to sway Henry in opposite directions by the vehemence of their
language (V.3).

Had he chosen to do so, Shakespeare could have written a very
different kind of play. He could easily have found the necessary material
in his sources. For example, there is the intrigue and the ambush which
resulted, in Holinshed, in Richard being taken captive to Flint Castle:
Shakespeare omits it all. Similarly, he leaves out the fighting of Richard's
Irish campaign completely. In other words, Shakespeare deliberately
reduced the action as much as possible. When he did add to his sources, it
was not to supply lively incidents but, in the scenes centred on the Queen
(II.2, III.4, V.1), to give himself the opportunity to explore the pathos and
sadness of Richard's situation.

Richard and Henry

Richard II is, then, an unusual history play in that it is not interested in
the political rivalries or military actions which are the common concern
of history plays. There are very few events in the play, and those few are
all arranged off-stage: Henry's invasion, Richard's actual agreement to
abdicate, the Abbot of Westminster's plot, the arrangements to kill
Richard, we see the *consequences* of all these but we see none of them

planned and only the last actually carried out. The interest of the play lies not in them: its focus is elsewhere, in a word, in Richard himself. Not even Henry, his successful rival, ever steals our attention.

Henry

In one sense, Henry is the hero of the play. After all, it is he who becomes Henry IV. However, we hardly think of him as a hero because Shakespeare depicts him in such a way that he can never rival our interest in Richard. Indeed, we hardly know Henry at all. He speaks well and imposingly in I.1 and I.3, but also very formally. While we do not doubt the sincerity of his desire to avenge Gloucester's death, we learn very little of his personal feelings. When Richard banishes him, Henry replies simply 'Your will be done' (I.3.144). There is no evidence of surprise, shock, dismay (contrast the reaction of Mowbray, I.3.154–73). This is characteristic of Henry throughout the play. He says very little, and never anything about his deepest thoughts and feelings. Richard, it seems, suspects Henry of ambition right from the start (I.1.109, I.3.129–32), but Henry, when he returns from banishment, insists that it is only to gain his rights as Duke of Lancaster (II.3.112–35). York, to whom this speech is addressed, recognises the justness of Henry's claim (II.1.187–99, II.2.111–15, II.3.140–1), but he too comes soon to suspect Henry of aiming at more than this (III.3.16–17). Henry similarly tells Richard at Flint Castle he wants only his rights (III.3.31–61, 107–20), but Richard remains convinced Henry is not telling the truth, and correctly foresees his deposition (III.3.143–59). But with all this suspicion about, we hear nothing from Henry about his real intentions. His first (and last) reference to the crown is the single, abrupt line in which he actually takes it: 'In God's name I'll ascend the regal throne' (IV.1.113). We simply do not know when he conceives this higher aim: whether it is what he always intended, or whether the ambition grew gradually. Similarly, we do not know what he intends to do as king, how he justifies his claim to the throne, or what his conception of kingship is.

With this reticence goes an extraordinary ease of accomplishment which we have noticed in the scene summaries and in the discussion of the plot. Henry seems to have to make no effort at all to organise an invasion, win support, or capture the King. At the end of III.1 he expects to fight the Welsh, but we know from II.4 that they have disbanded. This is typical: opposition there is none. Even Henry himself is surprised to find Richard at Flint so easily (III.3.20–6). He has literally stumbled on the King (and Shakespeare has deliberately arranged it so), and Richard then simply 'comes down' (III.3.178).

This has two effects. In the first place, Henry is not very interesting as a person. We simply do not know enough about him. At the end of the play, there are signs of anxiety and guilt (V.3.1–12, V.4.45–52), but these come after the taking of the throne. In the body of the play, it is Richard, not Henry, who holds our attention.

In the second place, Henry seems not to be directing events at all. Because Shakespeare tells us so little about his plans and intentions it seems that he has none, and he appears as a result to be someone for whom everything goes right by great good fortune. He simply lands in England, and the crown falls into his lap. We shall take this point further in a moment when we look at the tragedy: now we shall turn to the depiction of Richard.

Richard

Undoubtedly part of Shakespeare's intention in depicting Henry like this was to ensure that Richard should be the centre of the play. He is far more central than, for example, Edward in Marlowe's *Edward II* or Henry IV in Shakespeare's later plays. When we first read the play, we are struck by how much he says (especially in contrast to Henry), by how often he ponders on his feelings and tells us about his emotions. It is because of this that we come to feel sympathy for him. But the order in which Shakespeare chooses to reveal features of his character to us is still more important in winning our sympathy. We may say that our view of Richard passes through three stages: I.1–I.3; I.4–II.1; III.2–V.5.

(1) **I.1–I.3:** We first meet Richard in I.1 as 'every inch a king' (*King Lear*, IV.6.107). The monarch is, above all, the source of law and order, and in this capacity Richard is introduced. In dealing with the quarrel between Henry and Mowbray he speaks royally and powerfully. He appears to be, as he says, impartial (I.1.115–23), and when he orders the appellants to appear at Coventry he is obeyed (I.1.196–201). However, before we come to Coventry, I.2 is introduced and it very seriously qualifies the favourable impression Richard has made on us. From Gaunt we learn that Richard himself was involved in Gloucester's murder, the subject of the quarrel in the first scene (I.2.1–8, 38–41). In other words, far from being an impartial judge removed from the question at issue, Richard is himself implicated in it, far more deeply than his royal bearing might have led us to suppose.

Richard is not, however, involved merely as a guilty party. If we look back to I.1.104 we find Henry says that Gloucester's blood ran 'like sacrificing Abel's'. Abel was killed by his brother Cain, and the image suggests a close relationship between murderer and victim. And Gloucester was, of course, Richard's uncle. What seems like a stately and ceremonial occasion is, in fact, a family quarrel. As line 107 points out, Henry's grandfather Edward III is Richard's grandfather, and

Richard's round-about way of saying 'cousin' ('father's brother's son', line 117) only calls attention to the nearness of their relationship. In fact we see, in I.1, one cousin accusing a man of a murder for which, we learn in I.2, the other cousin was responsible. Richard, then, is not quite the king he seems—and he, perhaps feeling his guilt, already suspects Henry's motives and imagines he may be after his own throne (I.1.109, 115–7).

The realisation that Richard is involved in the quarrel helps us to understand why in I.3 Richard abruptly stops the contest and banishes both men. Both men are a threat to him. Mowbray knows the truth about Richard's involvement and so is dangerous (and he does seem very hurt by Richard's sentence, I.3.154–73). On the other hand, Richard suspects Henry of ambition, as we have just seen. He repeats the suspicion here (I.3.129–32), and returns to it in the next scene (I.4.20–36). So, by banishing both, he prevents Mowbray from revealing what he knows and (as he thinks) prevents Henry from achieving his ambition.

(2) **I.4–II.1:** We find, then, that after introducing Richard as a royal king, Shakespeare begins to introduce into our mind doubts about his kingly qualities. This process speeds up when we meet Richard in private with his flatterers in I.4. He has now (as he had in I.1 and I.3) no need to pretend, to act like a king, and the result is a remarkable come-down. We find he is petulant, resentful, callous, and prepared to act illegally to finance his Irish campaign. This revelation of what Richard is really like prepares us to believe the criticisms of him made by Gaunt in the next scene, II.1 (they are listed in the scene summary). And when, on Gaunt's death, Richard seizes his wealth and lands, all the suspicions that have been gathered are confirmed. Richard is a king without any of Gaunt's or York's sense of duty. He flouts the law and ignores criticism, with a blind disregard for the consequences. He plays the King, but acknowledges no bond between King and subject; he supposes he may banish Henry without consequence; farm his realm without any come-back; rob Gaunt with impunity. Gaunt had tried to warn him that such deeds were storing up trouble for the future (II.1.95–9), but in vain. When York's outburst actually shows Richard the effect his illegal actions have on loyal subjects, Richard is simply unable to grasp what is wrong. 'Why, uncle, what's the matter?' he says (II.2.186). It is this inability to see what is the matter—to realise that a king needs to deserve loyalty and support from his people—which brings about Richard's fall.

(3) **III.2–V.5:** When Richard sets off for Ireland, then, we have ample evidence that he is a bad king. And during the following scenes we see the consequences. Henry easily achieves power because the people love him

and not their king (the point is made repeatedly: I.4.20–36; II.1.246–8; III.2.112–20). It is a long time, however, before we meet Richard again. And when we do, in III.2, we know by the end of the scene that his position is hopeless. The effect of this is to separate the guilty king in the early part of the play from the man we meet later in the play. We must always remember that a drama works through time. We have been shown Richard's failings, and so can understand why he loses power. But now, having given our disgust at Richard's behaviour time to fade, Shakespeare introduces him as the victim of circumstances. From now on he will do all he can to arouse our sympathy for Richard. We may notice the following ways he does this:

(*i*) As we have seen, Richard's guilt and unpleasant behaviour are locked away at the beginning of the play. His follies are now rarely mentioned (notice that Richard does *not* confess publicly in IV.1 as Northumberland demands), so that we are now less impressed by his guilt than by his suffering.

(*ii*) That suffering now plays a major part as Richard repeatedly explores his agony of mind and spirit. His mental turmoil—not his failings as king—is the matter of his speeches in III.2, III.3, IV.1, V.1 and V.5, and so is what we notice.

(*iii*) And because Richard's guilt is now in the background, he appears as the victim of rebellion and betrayal. This is certainly his own view, which he presents by likening Henry and his followers to Judas and Pilate.

(*iv*) Shakespeare now gives to Richard some of his finest poetry to express himself, so that his thoughts and feelings are conveyed to us more hauntingly and powerfully than those of anyone else.

(*v*) Because of this, we come now to know Richard intimately, and so feel for him in his sorrow.

So we can see that Shakespeare has carefully arranged his presentation of Richard so that the audience, while recognising that he has been foolish and negligent, can feel sympathy for him in his suffering. It is not quite accurate to say that Richard is either a bad king who deserves to lose his throne or that he is an appealing figure cruelly and unjustly treated. Shakespeare presents him as both.

Tragedy

Character and circumstance

We all use the adjective 'tragic' casually in everyday speech when we wish to say that something is very unfortunate. In literary discussions, however, the word has a richer meaning. For a play (or novel) to be tragic in the full sense of the word it is not enough that it tells an unhappy story: it must provoke in us a particular kind of response, of which feeling sad is only a part. In Shakespearean tragedy certain features recur in the plays to create this response.

First of all, the play deals with a hero whom we admire in some way and for whom we feel sympathy. This is necessary so that we do feel sorry at what happens to him (which we would not if he were merely nasty) and regret that at his death so much that is good is lost. Shakespeare manages this by usually choosing a hero who holds a high position in the state (Hamlet, King Lear, Richard II), so that his death matters, and by revealing his character to us so that we come to know and respect him despite his faults.

Secondly, we first meet this hero in happy and successful circumstances, and then, through the course of the plot, he is brought to ruin and destruction. However, the way he is brought to death is important. A man who is merely the victim of bad luck is unlucky, but not tragic; a man who receives the punishment he deserves is justly, and not tragically, killed. A tragic fate is one which is both unlucky (the result of unfortunate circumstances) and deserved (the result of the hero's own failings), both unjust and just. As a result, the audience experiences a kind of tension: we feel the man should die, and should not die, at the same time.

We can see just this tragic irony and tension in *Richard II*. Richard is in many ways a bad man and a bad king, and, to that extent, he deserves to lose his throne. On the other hand, it is not his fault that of all men he should have Henry to deal with: it was, from Richard's point of view, very unlucky that he should choose to banish the one man determined enough to resist him. For that, of course, is Richard's tragic mistake: he expects to solve all his difficulties by banishing Henry and Mowbray, and achieves quite the opposite result. Another way of making the same point about the tragic combination of character and circumstance would be to say that Richard is a fine man but quite unsuited to be king: the tragedy results from his inability as a man to act properly in the situation in which he finds himself. Were he a capable king, he would be able to deal with Henry. It is a measure of Shakespeare's skill, and of the tragic tension of the play, that while we appreciate that Richard is at fault we yet cannot dismiss him as a foolish man who deserves his fate.

And while we feel sympathy for him as a man, we know he is a bad king.
That is precisely the dilemma a tragedy poses.

Inevitability

It is characteristic of Shakespearean tragedy that once the hero has made
his fatal mistake we feel an increasing sense of inevitability about the
outcome. In our play, this is one consequence of the way Shakespeare
presents Henry. As we saw a moment ago (p. 84), Henry seems not to
arrange things but to be carried along by good fortune. This sense of
men being powerless over their destinies is enforced by the many
references and images in the play which see the action as the irresistible
and inevitable workings of fortune. One of the earliest remarks of this
kind comes from the Queen just after Richard has left for Ireland:

> Yet again methinks
> Some unborn sorrow, ripe in fortune's womb
> Is coming towards me, and my inward soul
> With nothing trembles. At something it grieves
> More than with parting from my lord the King
> (II.2.9–13)

A pregnant woman must give birth: the image suggests that the
'something' the Queen fears will, must, make itself known. Similarly,
Green sees York's chances of withstanding Henry as nil:

> Alas, poor Duke! The task he undertakes
> Is numbering sands and drinking oceans dry.
> (II.2.144–5)

York is clearly helpless to change the course of events. Richard himself
uses a fatalistic image of inevitability: 'Down, down I come like
glistening Phaethon' (III.3.178). Richard can no more resist Henry than
Phaethon could withstand Zeus's thunderbolts. In the same way
Richard's image of the water buckets in the deposition scene suggests
that Henry's rise to power is inevitable, mechanical:

> Now is this golden crown like a deep well
> That owes two buckets, filling one another,
> The emptier ever dancing in the air,
> The other down, unseen, and full of water.
> That bucket down and full of tears am I,
> Drinking my griefs whilst you mount up on high.
> (IV.1.183–8)

If you fill one bucket, the other *must* rise.

Tragic loss

And lest we are in any danger of seeing Richard's fall not as tragic but as his just deserts for ruling badly, Shakespeare finally wins our sympathy to Richard, and gives the play a general tragic significance, by making it quite clear that, whatever justice Henry may claim on his side, when he does gain the throne something is lost. Richard, clearly, is a more kingly king: when Henry takes the throne, something splendid has gone. Richard was foolish, almost silly, certainly: Henry is more efficient; but he is also duller. The England celebrated by Gaunt (II.1.31–58) will not, we feel, have the same grandeur and romance under Henry. After all, his reign begins in Act IV with a very unseemly quarrel amongst his nobles, quite unlike the formal exchange of challenges (on the same issue, the death of Gloucester) which began the play. Shakespeare certainly intended the contrast to show the change which has come over the court. And Henry ends the play seemingly suddenly aged, worried, guilt-ridden: there is no triumph here.

This impression is strengthened by the many references to Edward III and his sons. The Duchess of Gloucester sets the tone of these references when she likens Edward's sons to 'seven vials of his sacred blood' (I.2.12). They were the true sons of a divinely appointed king. Repeatedly they are mentioned as a contrast in nobility, integrity and courage with the present times: they suggest England's glorious past (see, for example, York's recollection in II.3.98–104). When the play opens, only two, Gaunt and York, remain. After Gaunt's death, York is 'the last of noble Edward's sons' (II.1.171). We have a sense of a great race of princes dying out. Richard's behaviour as king betrays them, betrays his inheritance. Gaunt rebukes him like this:

> O, had thy grandsire with a prophet's eye
> Seen how his son's son should destroy his sons,
> From forth thy reach he would have laid thy shame,
> Deposing thee before thou wert possessed,
> Which art possessed now to depose thyself.
>
> (II.1.104–8)

York repeats the charge later in the scene (II.1.171–84)

And with Richard's death the last chance to regain this nobility is lost. Richard was the last king to rule in direct succession from William the Conqueror: after him, the crown would go to the strongest. In other words, the fruitfulness of the Duchess's other image for Edward's sons, 'seven fair branches springing from one root' (I.2.13) is lost: the tree withers and dies.

Tragic gain

This leads to a final point about Shakespearean tragedy. In a strange way we always feel that it is better that the hero dies. This is partly because, through his suffering, he comes to know himself and the world better: he has grown in stature. So, in our play, Richard in V.5 shows a new kind of self-knowledge and a new dignity in adversity. He can now admit he has been wrong (V.5.41–9), when at the start of the play he had reacted with anger or incredulity to criticism (II.1.115–23, 186). He can now meditate on his sorrow without the emotional instability and excess he had shown in III.2. There is also, in a Shakespearean tragedy, the feeling that the hero could not feel at home in the world of the end of the play, and hence a certain relief that he has died. There would have been no future for Richard as the vassal of Henry. Far better he should die, a still glorious, if misguided, king, than that he should live on doing what Henry tells him. That would be to be less, not more, of a man than he is. It is because of these two characteristics that a Shakespearean tragedy is never wholly sad: something has been gained.

Themes

Richard II is a play arranged clearly around the loss of power by one man and the gaining of it by another. Yet we cannot simply admire the man who gains it, nor condemn the man who loses it. We know too little about Henry and we feel too much sympathy for Richard for this. But then neither can we simply blame the man who takes it and respect the man who loses it. Henry has been too grievously wronged and Richard committed too many extravagant and illegal acts for this. In other words, we cannot take clear sides.

The theme of *Richard II* is kingship. Time and again characters discuss the rights and duties of a king and the rights and duties of a subject, and yet the play refuses to choose between them. Its richness derives from the fact that Shakespeare does not take a dogmatic line on the issues raised. He finds pros and cons on both sides of the central conflict.

Richard's majesty

Shakespeare is well able to detect failings in his king. Gaunt (whose character is such that we trust him) directly implicates Richard in Gloucester's murder and later charges him with this (I.2.1–8, II.1.124–31). His brother York is of the same mind (II.1.165). We know of Richard's shortcomings as king (II.1.93–114, 163–70, III.4.48–66) and we see his despicable behaviour upon Henry's banishment and Gaunt's death (I.4, II.1.153–233). And yet there is no doubt in the play

but that Richard is true king. Gaunt himself, more conscious of
Richard's guilt and unworthiness than anyone else, refuses to act against
him for this very reason:

> God's is the quarrel; for God's substitute,
> His deputy anointed in His sight,
> Hath caused his death; the which if wrongfully,
> Let heaven revenge, for I may never lift
> An angry arm against His minister.   (I.2.37–41)

Gaunt here expresses the contemporary Tudor view of kingship: that a
divinely appointed king is answerable only to God and cannot be
challenged or judged by his subjects. To the Elizabethans, therefore,
rebellion was a most heinous offence. The Bishop of Carlisle puts the
same point yet more strongly at the very moment that the King is about
to be deposed (IV.1.114–49). There can be no doubt that Shakespeare
wanted his audience to be very much alive to the horror of what Henry is
about to do. He has always allowed Richard majesty—York had
remarked at Flint:

> Yet looks he like a king. Behold, his eye,
> As bright as is the eagle's, lightens forth
> Controlling majesty. Alack, alack for woe
> That any harm should stain so fair a show.   (III.3.68–71)

In the deposition scene itself Shakespeare works to remind us of this
majesty, so that we not only sympathise with Richard but are fully aware
that he is rightfully king. Richard's reference to the sufferings and trial of
Christ bring together several strands in Shakespeare's portrayal.
Richard is a divinely appointed king (as Christ's mission on earth was
divinely ordained), betrayed by those in whom he placed his trust (as
Christ by Judas) and deposed by a process which pretends to be legal
while those responsible claim to be innocent (as Christ was tried by
Pilate). Richard reproves Northumberland for asking him to read a list
of his crimes, saying that Northumberland would not like to recite *his*:

> If thou wouldst
> There shouldst thou find one heinous article,
> Containing the deposing of a king
> And cracking the strong warrant of an oath,
> Marked with a blot, damned in the book of heaven.
> Nay, all of you that stand and look upon me,
> Whilst that my wretchedness doth bait myself,
> Though some of you—with Pilate—wash your hands,
> Showing an outward pity, yet you Pilates
> Have here delivered me to my sour cross,
> And water cannot wash away your sin.   (IV.1.231–41)

There can be no doubt of the sanctity of Richard's kingship nor of the sympathy we are meant to feel for him. And feeling that we must share, at least in part, the Bishop of Carlisle's horror at the deposition.

Henry's wrongs

On the other hand, there is no doubt that this same king wrongs Henry grievously. We actually see him do it, with a horrible callousness. The prospect provokes York to an impassioned plea to Richard. York realises that if Richard seizes Henry's inheritance as Duke of Lancaster he undercuts the very foundations of society and dangerously weakens his own position as king:

> Take Hereford's rights away, and take from Time
> His charters and his customary rights.
> Let not tomorrow then ensue today.
> Be not thyself; for how art thou a king
> But by fair sequence and succession?
>
> (II.1.195–9)

Richard disregards this, and the warning that follows, with the blind wilfulness characteristic of him earlier in the play. But we—the audience—cannot disregard it. Just as Shakespeare gave full weight to the sanctity of Richard's kingship, so he gives full weight to the grievance which provokes Henry. We know and admire Gaunt: this makes our horror at Richard's act, carried out only moments after Gaunt has died warning him against his folly, and carried out against Gaunt's heir, the more horrible. And it is followed immediately by York's plea. York, too, is ignored. It is not coincidence that in these very passages Shakespeare chooses to remind us of Edward III (II.1.124–38, 171–83). The point is clear: here is Richard turning his back on—betraying—the nobility of the Plantagenet kings.

Furthermore, Henry, though a reticent figure, never behaves with the pettiness or meanness of Richard. He may not be an attractive man, but he has a cool authority. He can grant Aumerle a pardon in V.3 (unlike Richard in I.1 and I.3, Henry is not implicated in the guilt of his nobles) and certainly never intends to murder Richard. Shakespeare could easily have discredited Henry's position by making him an unsavoury, unscrupulous or petty character. He does not do this. Richard regards Henry's popular following with scorn (I.4. 23–36), but it does not seem contemptible to an audience. On the contrary, it is Richard's scorn which is contemptible. Richard ignores his subjects. Secure in his divine right, he does not need their favour and seems to have no sense that he owes it to them to rule in their best interests. Henry does pay attention to others, to common people, and (for aught we know to the contrary) deserves their admiration. Certainly, it is the people's affection for Henry which renders Richard's position hopeless (III.2.112–20).

The central dilemma

There is, then, right and wrong on both sides: on the one hand the divinely appointed king who ignores his people; on the other, the man of justice who enjoys popular support but who has no claim to the throne. It is in this respect that York is so significant in the play. In him we see exactly this dilemma:

> Both are my kinsmen
> T'one is my sovereign, whom both my oath
> And duty bids defend. T'other again
> Is my kinsman, whom the King hath wronged,
> Whom conscience and my kindred bids to right   (II.2.111—15)

We may, then conclude that Shakespeare does full justice to the authority of Richard's kingship and to Richard's failings; to the wrongs Henry suffers and to the injustice of what he does to Richard. He refuses to say, dogmatically, either that a king should not be judged or that Henry was right to act against Richard. If there is a final verdict in the play, it seems to be that the affair is a mystery. We have seen how the planning of the action makes things appear to happen almost without human effort (p. 84); we have seen how Richard's guilt (the cause of events, if there is one) is separated from his suffering (the effect of his wrongdoing) so that in the theatre we tend to forget the follies and see Richard as the victim of circumstances he was powerless to prevent (p. 88); and we have seen how the imagery stresses the inevitability of the action (p. 89). All this together seems to support York's verdict: 'But heaven hath a hand in these events' (V.2.37).

Style

Word-play

Richard II was clearly written by a man who was alive to the ambiguities of words, the different senses they carry, and who wished to *use* these senses. When we write or talk we try to say as precisely as we can what we mean. Shakespeare, by contrast, seems often to want to carry on several meanings at once, and does not seem at all concerned to choose between them, to write clearly and exactly. A poet is someone who is aware of the suggestiveness of words, but, of all poets, Shakespeare is the one who is most aware of the nuances and ambiguities of words. Instead of shunning it, he delights in it and tries to use it. He does not tie words down: he releases them. He uses words with a kind of abandon, a joy in them merely as words, as things to play with. This can be very disconcerting for the reader unaccustomed to this taste, especially when it is an early play which is being read, where this trait is most apparent.

We notice this aspect of Shakespeare's style most plainly in his word-play. This is something which is likely to disturb a modern reader. We can accept the comic use of puns and quibbles (for example, in the conversation of Benedick and Beatrice in *Much Ado About Nothing*), but *Richard II*, unusually for a Shakespeare play, has no comedy in it. We find it much more difficult to accept verbal ingenuity at serious moments, such as this play offers us. A conspicuous example occurs early on when the dying Gaunt puns on his name (II.1.72–83). We can see that this is ingenious, and it does stress Gaunt's age and anguish, but we may well feel its elaborateness prevents us from taking it as a sincere expression of feeling. Yet Shakespeare actually calls our attention to this ingenuity when Richard exclaims 'Can sick men play so nicely with their names?' (II.1.84). Again, at the very moment of Richard's submission to Henry, Shakespeare has the King making puns:

> Down, down I come like glistening Phaethon,
> Wanting the manage of unruly jades.
> In the base-court—base-court, where kings grow base
> To come at traitors' calls, and do them grace.   (III.3.178–81)

Here, an everyday technical term ('base-court') becomes suggestive of the moral treachery which is taking place ('where kings grow base'), so that Richard's actual descent from the walls of Flint Castle become an action symbolising his descent from high and noble office to ignominy and shame.

The use of word-play at such serious moments as these implies that Shakespeare must have felt it an effective way to convey meaning. Once we have learned to allow more than one sense to be present in our mind at once, we can still often see how this might be so. In II.1.30 York tries to dissuade Gaunt from speaking to Richard because he has not the strength: 'Tis breath thou lackest and that breath wilt thou lose'. Both parts of this line carry two senses: Gaunt 'lacks breath' because his illness makes him short of breath and because, since he is dying, he has not many more breaths to breathe; he will 'lose' his breath both by using it up in speaking and by wasting it since Richard will pay no attention. The compression here stresses both Gaunt's dire position and the futility of what he hopes to do. Then Gaunt replies:

> Methinks I am a prophet new-inspired,
> And thus, expiring, do foretell of him   (II.1.31–2)

Gaunt takes up the idea of breathing and, by manipulating it (or, rather, having Shakespeare manipulate it for him), manages to express himself more succinctly, more pointedly than would otherwise be the case. This is proved by the fact that, when dealing with such a passage as this, we often cannot give a single modern equivalent, but can only suggest the several meanings present. So here: Gaunt is dying—the breath of life is leaving him—and yet he chooses to use up the breath remaining to him to prophesy of Richard. As he approaches death, he feels himself possessed of new insights, as though inspired. It is as though a vision has been breathed into him by God. This vision he will now give out again, as he breathes it out in words, and as he dies. The word-play here accentuates the awesomeness of Gaunt's words (they are 'given' to him to say) and his resolute commitment to truth (he will die saying them). The passage also underlines the futility of using breath on (talking to) Richard. York will experience this shortly when Richard responds to his passionate outcry, 'Why, uncle, what's the matter?' (II.1.186).

Rhyme

This play makes much more use of rhyme than Shakespeare's later plays, and does not use prose. This contributes to our sense that it is a very 'poetic' play. We can see the rhyme serving several functions: all of them derive from the fact that we *notice* rhyme sounds when we hear characters speaking; and so they call attention to what is being said. So rhyme marks the end of scenes or an exit (I.2.204–8, II.1.211–14). It signals a significant moment, like a leave-taking (I.3.93–6) and, used at length, can stress the formality and ritualistic quality of a scene (I.1.158–95). It is used to stress a point (I.1.41–6), to conclude a speech with emphasis (I.2.54–5), to show that a statement allows no contradiction (I.3.197–8), and to mark out a pointed saying (I.1.156–7, II.1.7–8, IV.1.200–1). When rhyme sounds echo between characters, even though they may be disagreeing, it serves to link them and what they are saying and so underlines that in some way they depend upon each other's reactions (IV.1.189–90, 193–4). All these are forms of emphasis: the student may easily find additional examples of his own.

Long speeches

We begin to see that Shakespeare's drama is deliberately poetic. He uses words openly for effect. This is most marked in the longer speeches, which, in our play, are all like set pieces. We have noticed how little action there is in the play (p. 83). To a greater extent than in most Shakespeare plays, the centre of interest lies in what people say in exchanges made up of long speeches which, through imagery and word-play, develop an argument or explore emotion. There is only one real soliloquy in the play (that is, a speech spoken by a character alone on the stage), at the beginning of V.5, but many of the speeches, although supposedly addressed to some one, have the quality of soliloquies in that the person speaking seems more interested in exploring his own thoughts than in communicating with another. Gaunt's England speech in II.1.31–68 is an example, and so are Richard's speeches in III.2. Even in the deposition scene, Richard is not really engaged in dialogue. The speech to the mirror (IV.1.275–90) is a private meditation, even though the stage is filled with courtiers. In contrast to these are those more orderly and logical speeches, such as Gaunt's rebukes to Richard (II.1.93–114, 124–38), Henry's account to York of his aims (II.3.112–35), and the Bishop of Carlisle's address (IV.1.114–49), which are directed to persuading some one else to a course of action. Yet we are still a long way from ordinary conversation: it is rather impassioned debate we hear.

Imagery

The extraordinary richness and variety of the imagery again marks out *Richard II* as an earlier play, but it also shows Shakespeare trying to work on our emotions. The images do not merely illustrate the points the characters are making; they affect us so that we respond with more than our minds. When Gaunt likens England to Eden (II.1.42) he brings to bear on our conception of England all the associations of Eden— perfection, happiness, a place created specially by God for the well-being of men. We may say that the image here is a kind of short-hand (one word brings in a great deal) and that we may list the points it makes: but it is the emotional response which counts. To say, simply, that England was perfect is not nearly so affecting, because we respond only with our mind to this proposition.

The student can find other examples for himself, but we should notice that throughout this play Shakespeare makes use of a small group of recurrent images. By this means he underlines the themes of the play and gives to the drama a distinctive quality. Thus, the repeated references to blood remind us of the cruelty and treachery that are not very far from the splendid world of Richard's court. The many allusions to Edward III and his sons (often linked with the blood imagery) prevent us from forgetting the Plantaganet nobility betrayed in Richard. Images of youth and age underline Richard's inexperience, and images of death and the grave haunt the play, darkening its atmosphere. One of the richest of these images is that of the sun. This is an appropriate image since the sun formed part of Richard's own badge, but Shakespeare uses it to suggest the splendour of Richard's kingship and, since the sun is the most important body in the sky and its light a traditional image for

God's grace, his conception of the divinity of a king. Conversely, night and darkness convey the loss of this splendour, the absence and fall of the King. The image of the garden and images of tears and grief are as common.

We may end by noticing one very suggestive group of such images and allusions. In many of his plays Shakespeare actually discusses language and its powers. *Richard II* is no exception. Indeed, the characters are unusually aware of both the influence and deceptiveness of words, and make many remarks which raise questions about the relationship between speech and action, words and truth. Mowbray sees his banishment in terms of loss of the occasion to use English (I.3.159–73); Gaunt's death is reported by Northumberland as a loss of words, 'His tongue is now a stringless instrument' (II.1.149). In each case this is fitting, since Mowbray had tried to defend himself with words and Gaunt to reform Richard with words. Henry calls attention to the power of a king's words (I.3.213–15) and Richard's loss of power is seen when he literally eats his own kingly words (III.3.133–6). But if words can sway, they can also deceive: the Duchess of York does not believe her husband sincere in demanding Aumerle's death (V.3.101), and York himself points to the false words of Richard's favourites (II.1.17–26). And words are limited too: we are reminded they cannot express the deepest feelings when the faithful groom says to Richard 'What my tongue dares not, that my heart shall say' (V.5.97). As that line suggests, they are also dangerous things: Ross is afraid to speak his mind (II.1.228–9) and the Abbot of Westminster swears the conspirators to silence (IV.1.327–8).

It is, at times, almost as if the characters are themselves aware that they are part of a literary work, that they are part of a story. They can call attention to details of technique: so Richard begins his soliloquy at Pomfret by explaining the metaphorical method he has adopted: 'I have been studying how I may compare/This prison where I live unto the world' (V.5.1–2). More often, they liken their experience to that of fictional characters. Gaunt speaks of his 'death's sad tale' (II.1.16), Richard sees himself as like those kings whose deaths are recounted in 'sad stories' (III.2.156), and he speaks of kings as mere actors playing a part (III.2.160–70). On his way to imprisonment he sees his life as a 'lamentable tale' (V.1.44), and his murderer speaks of his crime as 'chronicled in hell' (V.5.116). York tells his wife 'the story' of Richard and Henry's entrance into London (V.2.1–3). Taken together, references and images like these increase our sense that we are watching a mysterious pageant (IV.1.320) in which people play the part assigned to them until the 'antic' Death comes to claim them (III.2.162).

Characters

Richard and Henry and their followers

The characters of Richard and Henry have been dealt with earlier in this Commentary, on pages 83 to 87. The chief figures in *Richard II* are, of course, Richard Plantagenet and Henry Bolingbroke. With Richard are associated his 'flatterers', the 'caterpillars of the commonwealth' (II.3.165, III.4.40–7), Bushy, Bagot and Green. These characters are not individualised but serve to represent those favourites who, in the opinion of his critics, have misled Richard (II.1.100, 241–2; III.1.8–10). All that is necessary for the play is that they should be young (like Richard himself), unpleasant (Richard's behaviour in I.4 must be familiar and acceptable to them) and unheroic (as they are in II.2.122–48), so that we feel they get their just deserts in III.1. With them is linked Aumerle (see I.4), but he is a more fully realised character, loyal to Richard until the discovery of the Abbot of Westminster's plot in Act V. Against these not very attractive figures are placed the wise old councillor, Gaunt, the staunch Bishop of Carlisle, and the Queen, for whom Richard is primarily a man, not a king. For the flatterers, of course, Richard is only a king, a source of wealth and influence, whom they desert as soon as the going gets rough.

Henry has fewer followers; indeed, only two of any note: the bluff Earl of Northumberland, who has little patience with Richard's elaborate speeches and high-strung emotions, and his son, Harry Percy, whose vigorous youth contrasts with the rather weak immaturity we associate with the flatterers and which Richard himself at times displays. However, with the down-to-earth character of Henry, these two are sufficient to give Henry's party the appearance of being composed of no-nonsense, practical and brave people, unlike Richard's unstable and flighty followers. The two groups are linked by York, the uncle of both Richard and Henry, who, in the course of the play, changes his allegiance from the one to the other.

Gaunt

John of Gaunt, Duke of Lancaster, appears in only four of the first five scenes of the play, but he plays a significant role in the scheme of the drama. He is an old man (who, of course, actually dies in II.1), a link with the great king, his father, Edward III. Herein lies his significance: in him lives the tradition of England's glorious past, and we see in Richard's scornful remarks (I.4.59–64, II.4.115–23) how little respect the present king pays it. In these early scenes of the play we hear from this noble man criticism of Richard which is quite disinterested. That is the crucial point: Henry has a grievance against Richard and we might expect him to oppose the King. Gaunt, however, is prepared to put aside personal feelings when trying to do what is best for his country (and so, though as a father he bitterly regrets it, as a councillor he agrees to the banishment of his son because he believes it to be in the interest of peace in England, I.3.233–46). He speaks against Richard not out of personal malice but out of love for his country. His famous speech in II.1.31–68 serves to conjure up in the mind of the audience early in the play a vision of England as an especially blessed land which has a lasting effect upon its view of the actions and of Richard's misdeeds. And Gaunt is constant in his opposition to the King's wrongdoings. Not only is he prepared to go to his death trying to reform the King, but, we gather from II.1.15, he has spent the earlier years of the King's reign in the same endeavour.

And yet, such is Gaunt's commitment to his duty as he sees it that he refuses to act against Richard himself, deeply as he feels the injustice of the murder of his brother Gloucester (I.2.1–8, 37–41). It is not for him to try to dethrone God's appointed deputy on earth. Unlike his son, Henry, he will place his trust in God to right matters; unlike his brother, York, however, he will resolutely and fearlessly oppose what he sees as the King's neglect of his duty; and, unlike his nephew, Richard, he will put the good of England before all else. In these ways he offers us a model of nobility against which we measure the other characters in the play, and all of them we find wanting.

York

Edmund of Langley, Duke of York, is Gaunt's brother and the last of Edward III's sons (II.1.171). He is both like and unlike his brother. He is like him in his absolute commitment to his duty. Richard recognises this loyalty for, just after York has rebuked him passionately and left the stage in disgust, he still makes the Duke governor of England in his absence (II.1.220–1). Later in the play, when he has taken an oath of allegiance to the new King Henry IV, York maintains his loyalty to him even to the point of sacrificing his own son Aumerle (V.3.53–72). We are not surprised to find Henry seeing in his uncle York something of his own father Gaunt (II.3.112–21), for York, like Gaunt, lets neither family nor personal considerations come before duty.

And yet York is a much less commanding figure than Gaunt. In him old age means not (as in Gaunt) the wisdom of experience and the courage of resolution. On the contrary, it means weakness, indecision and helplessness. It is York himself who tries to dissuade Gaunt from criticising the King lest it do more harm than good (II.1.3–4, 17–30) and, though he does make some efforts to organise resistance to Henry, these efforts are rather half-hearted (II.2.98–121). When York does meet Henry, he simply admits he is powerless (II.3.151–6). He is a man without either natural authority or initiative. Affairs simply leave him confused. So, from being Richard's governor, he comes to claim to be neutral (II.3.157–8). He feels sympathy for Richard (III.3.68–71), but he has moved from his neutrality to Henry's side by the time of the deposition and is the first to hail the new King (IV.1.107–12). By V.2.39 he has taken an oath of allegiance to Henry IV. It seems that, for all his sense of duty, he drifts with—or is pushed by—events. We have the impression that he is simply unable to cope, 'Things past redress are now with me past care' (II.3.170).

But we must not dismiss York as merely silly and ineffectual. In him is seen the central dilemma of the play, which Gaunt, fortunately, died before having to face. York has outlived his time. His simple but firm sense of duty, ideal when the King is strong and noble like Edward III, does not know which way to turn when the King is weak and negligent like Richard. It is precisely because York both wants to remain loyal to Richard and yet recognises he has not behaved as a king should to Henry that he is caught between the two sides (II.2.111–5). We might say that in him we see the confusion that results when the King ceases to be the true ruler and inspiration of his people.

Aumerle

We might think that Edward of York, Duke of Aumerle, is made of sterner stuff than his father, York. He refutes the charge of being involved in Gloucester's murder with courage and defiance (IV.1.8–85). He is prepared to take part in the Abbot of Westminster's plot to restore Richard to the throne (IV.1.323–4), and so does seem to have a stronger commitment to the old king than his father. On the other hand, his behaviour in I.4.1–19, where he speaks sneeringly of Henry after having seemed to behave affectionately to him in I.3.249–50, places him in the company of Richard's unpleasant followers. And when the Abbot's plot is discovered by York, he is ready enough to take his mother's advice and seek Henry's pardon (V.2.112–4, V.3.29–31). In just the same way, Richard's other companions had tried to save their own skins when in danger (II.2.122–40). In Aumerle we see a loyal, but not very noble, adherent of Richard's party.

Northumberland

Henry Percy, Earl of Northumberland, typifies Henry's followers as Aumerle does Richard's. The clearest trait in his character is down-to-earth realism. At the end of II.1 he has full knowledge of Henry's preparations for invasion and is resolute in acting quickly to join him. It is from him (as York notices) that we get the first hint that there is little respect for Richard's kingship amongst Henry's adherents (III.3.5–17). As this might lead us to expect, he has small patience with Richard's long speeches in the deposition scene. Richard sees himself as the victim of unjust betrayal; Northumberland is concerned only to prevent Richard from presenting himself as a martyr by having him confess publicly his crimes (IV.1.221–71). It is the same disregard for higher things which enables him promptly to arrest the Bishop of Carlisle after his speech in defence of Richard (IV.1.150–3). Northumberland is not a man to be swayed from his purpose by either exhibitions of emotional suffering or idealistic arguments about duty. In this respect, he typifies the no-nonsense, practical approach of Henry and his party.

Richard calls him the 'ladder' by which Henry ascends to the throne (V.1.55). Although Shakespeare pays little attention to the details of Henry's rise we can trace the steps Northumberland takes on his behalf.

(*i*)   He rallies the lords to side with Henry (II.1.224–300).

(*ii*) He accompanies Henry after he has landed at Ravenspurgh (II.3).

(*iii*) He executes Richard's favourites on Henry's orders (III.1.35).

(*iv*) At Flint Castle he is Henry's envoy to Richard (III.3.31–4, 101–20, 142, 176–7).

(*v*)   He arrests the Bishop of Carlisle and tries to make Richard confess his crimes (IV.1.150–3, 221–71).

(*vi*) He sends Richard to Pomfret and the Queen to France (V.1.52–5).

(*vii*) He successfully breaks up the conspiracy against Henry (V.6.6–10).

In short, no one is more active on Henry's behalf than he; no one is more single-minded and efficient in carrying through a plan. And yet no one is more dangerous as an ally, for, with his insensitivity to questions of conscience, morality and loyalty ('My guilt be on my head, and there an end' is how he abruptly dismisses them in V.1.69), Northumberland can hardly be trusted. It is no surprise to find that, as Richard prophesies (V.1.55–68), in the *Henry IV* plays he rebels against Henry when he finds it in his interest to do so. This man of affairs is an excellent foil to Richard's hopelessly inept idealism and York's weak irresolution.

Percy

Northumberland's son Harry Percy will, as 'Hotspur', play a large part in *1 Henry IV*, but his role in *Richard II* is slight. Our main impression is of a vigorous and brave young man, full of promise and far more purposeful (II.3.41–4) than either Richard's followers or the son Henry mentions at the beginning of V.3. This is the Prince Hal who will be Harry's rival in *1 Henry IV*.

Bishop of Carlisle

Thomas Merke, Bishop of Carlisle, is the noblest of Richard's followers, absolutely dedicated to his king. He is prepared to defend Richard in the midst of the enemy camp in IV.1. and to fight to restore him to his throne (IV.1.320–33, V.6.19–23). Despite his part in the Abbot of Westminster's plot, Henry, his enemy, grants him his life, but we do not feel that, like Aumerle, he would ever have changed his allegiance and begged for a pardon (V.6.24–7). Henry does this nevertheless because, as he says, 'High sparks of honour in thee have I seen' (V.6.29). There is similar evidence of his holiness and dignity earlier in the play when Percy says that there is in Flint Castle with Richard 'a clergyman/of holy reverence', and from this description Northumberland recognises the Bishop (III.3.27–30). To this bishop Shakespeare gives the most eloquent defence of Richard's rights as king (IV.1.114–31), but we should also notice that in III.2.27–32 the Bishop advises Richard to take steps to defend himself. Clearly, the Bishop is not an ecclesiastic ignorant of the ways of the world. He believes that 'heaven helps those who help themselves' (and he himself acts in the plot against Henry). That this high-minded clergyman, so unlike Richard's flatterers and the brusque Earl of Northumberland, should foretell bloody civil war as the consequence of Richard's deposition, leads us to believe this will indeed be the result (IV.1.132–49). Though the Bishop speaks seldom, when he does speak it is always pointedly and with good reason.

Queen Isabel

In the theatre of Shakespeare's day the parts of women were played by boys. This does not seem to have restricted Shakespeare much in his conception of his female characters—Rosalind in *As You Like It*, Beatrice in *Much Ado About Nothing* and Cleopatra in *Antony and Cleopatra* are examples of parts which actresses find challenging and are proud to take on. However, there is a recurrent kind of female character in the plays which may have derived from the fact that boys were to perform it. This is the figure of a beautiful young woman of innocence and simplicity. It is not a character with great range, and so does not demand too much of its performer. Miranda in *The Tempest*, for example, has an almost child-like directness and credulity. In the tragedies, this character, caught up in a situation she is powerless to influence, becomes a passive figure of pathos: such are Ophelia in *Hamlet* and Desdemona in *Othello*.

The Queen in *Richard II* belongs in this company. She has a gentleness which contrasts with Richard's heartless attitude to Gaunt (II.1.71) and a simplicity which can hope that, in the cruel world of power politics, she might be allowed to stay with Richard after his fall (V.1.83–7). As Richard says, 'That were some love, but little policy' (V.1.84). Hers is a world of love: the world of Henry and Northumberland a world of expedient policy.

Above all, perhaps, it is her helplessness we notice. In II.2 she anticipates fearfully something in the future she cannot understand because she is excluded from the world of men. In III.4 she overhears from another that Richard is in Henry's power. In V.1, at the end of it all, she comes to see again the husband whose fortunes she has had no part in. She is a choric figure: in these scenes, by exploring her emotions, Shakespeare deepens our sense of the pathos and tragedy of what happens to Richard. He creates a tender and loving relationship (remember he has deliberately made the Queen older than she was to do this, and we see the effect of what happens to Richard on one who loves him as a man, more dearly and intimately than anyone loved him as a king. That she should so cry out, in haunting and evocative lines, at the change in him, increases our awareness of what he has suffered (V.1.8–15), just as her earlier experience of a 'nameless woe' increased our apprehension (II.2.1–40).

Part 4

Hints for study

WE HAVE SEEN THAT, as the product of the English Renaissance, written for the Elizabethan stage, *Richard II* has a very distinctive character. It is quite unlike the writing with which we are familiar today. Only by recognising this can we begin to discuss the play in a worthwhile way. So we should do all we can to understand Shakespeare's method, so that we do not deliver criticisms which are ill-informed and unjust because they miss the point.

Our appreciation should try to be as inclusive as possible. The best understanding of a literary text is the one which can most satisfactorily explain all the features of the work. So we need to try to get as clear a view as we can of what *kind* of play we think this is, and then endeavour to see how each aspect of it fits in with this view. For example, if we think this is a play about a power struggle between two men, why do we learn so little of Henry? If we believe we are to sympathise with Richard, why does Shakespeare present him in such a poor light early in the play? It is the firmness of the overall grasp of the play which determines the merit of any discussion of, or essay on, it.

As these examples show, it is by asking questions that our understanding of a literary work grows. It is a good plan to pause frequently as we read to ask ourselves questions like: 'why does Shakespeare introduce this character here?'; 'why does he follow the last scene with this one?'; 'what would be the effect of this passage in the theatre?'; 'why do I feel like this when reading these lines?'. If we fail to ask such questions, we will find that we have drawn little from our reading. The play may have affected us, but we will be unable to say how or why.

Questions

The following are examples of the kind of questions on the play a student may expect to meet. They have all been touched on in these Notes, and considering them may help the reader to get clear in his own mind how he thinks the play works.

Structure and plot

---

(1) Analyse Shakespeare's presentation of any turning point in the play, and discuss its function in the play as a whole.

(2) Discuss, and illustrate with specific examples, the ways in which Shakespeare handles his sources to achieve dramatic effect.
(3) Why is there so little action in the play?
(4) Would you agree that Shakespeare makes Henry's success appear too easily achieved?
(5) Illustrate some of the ways in which the nature of the Elizabethan stage has affected the structure of the play.

Tragedy

(6) What do you understand to be the nature of Shakespearean tragedy? Illustrate your answer from *Richard II*.
(7) How far is Richard responsible for his own fate?
(8) Discuss the significance of foreboding in the play.
(9) Analyse the ways in which Shakespeare makes the outcome of the action appear inevitable. Do they increase, or detract from, the tragedy?
(10) Is *Richard II* a pessimistic play?

Themes

(11) Why does Shakespeare remind us so often of Edward III and his noble sons?
(12) How convincing do you find Richard's claim that 'The breath of worldly men cannot depose/The deputy elected by the Lord'?
(13) Discuss the significance of the Bishop of Carlisle's speech in Act IV.
(14) Does Shakespeare intend us to approve of Henry's action in taking the crown?
(15) What is the thematic relevance of III.4?

Style

(16) Discuss, and give examples of, the variety of Shakespeare's verse in the play.
(17) Discuss the merits and demerits of Shakespeare's use of word-play.
(18) Analyse one of the following speeches: II.1.31–68; III.2.144–77; IV.1.114–49; V.5.1–66. Assess the effectiveness of the significant features of the speech through your analysis and relate the speech to the wider concerns of the play.
(19) Examine the ways in which Shakespeare repeats and develops images through the play, and consider what is achieved by this technique.
(20) What functions does rhyme serve in the play?

Characters

(21) Analyse Shakespeare's depiction of Richard.
(22) Do you find Shakespeare's portrayal of Henry successful?
(23) Describe the character of York and explain his importance in the play.
(24) Would you agree that the characters are all, essentially, types?
(25) Why does Shakespeare introduce the characters of Gaunt and Queen Isabel? Consider particularly the ways in which his characterisation of them departs from his sources.

These questions have been divided up like the Commentary in these Notes, but we should always remember that categories like 'structure' and 'theme' only exist for the convenience of critical discussion. They are not separate things in the text itself. That is a single whole, and so we find that any one of our convenient categories will always lead to another. For example, Richard's contribution to the theme of the play depends upon what kind of person he is, and that in turn depends upon the sequence in which, through his handling of the action, Shakespeare has chosen to reveal aspects of his character to us. Here, theme, characterisation and plot all combine. We must try to remember that a work of art is an organic whole like this. Indeed, we can say that the more completely satisfying the work, the more difficult it will be to isolate any one particular feature of it from the others. It is only in bad writing that the rhymes, let us say, are painfully obvious. But we do have to distinguish different aspects of a text if we wish to talk about it. The categories used in the Commentary should help the reader to pinpoint the main features of *Richard II*.

In preparing answers to questions like those given above, we need both to marshal our points in an orderly way and to support them with references to, and quotations from, the text. The reasons for this are simple: only if we present our points in an orderly fashion will our argument make sense, and only if we bring forward our evidence can we prove that our argument is sound. Without order, no sense of the play as a work of art can be conveyed: without quotations, our views lack conviction—there is no proof. A safe plan to follow in essays is (*i*) explain our understanding of the question; (*ii*) explain how we intend to deal with it; (*iii*) follow through this programme in order; (*iv*) conclude what we have established. This will ensure that the reader of the essay knows what we are trying to do.

References

As far as quotations are concerned, most of the significant lines in *Richard II* have been mentioned in the course of these Notes. For convenience, some of them are listed below: the reader may like to look them up as a revision exercise to see whether he can explain their significance; help should be found in the relevant section of the Commentary and the scene summaries.

Key scenes: I.1; I.3; II.1; III.3; IV.1; V.5

Scenes involving Richard: I.1; I.3; I.4; II.1; III.2; IV.1; V.1; V.5

Scenes involving Henry: I.1; I.3; II.3; III.1; III.3; IV.1; V.3; V.6

Choric scenes involving the Queen: II.2.1–72; III.4; V.1

Rhyme: I.1.18–19, 41–6, 82–3, 107–8, 122–3, 150–1, 154–95, 200–5; I.2.54–5, 69–74; I.3.55–62, 64–8, 93–8, 144–7, 172–7, 206–7, 214–5, 221–52, 292–3, 302–5, 308–9; II.1.13–16, 29–30, 137–40, 143–6, 149–54, 209–14, 297–300; II.2.31–2, 120–1, 141–2, 145–8; II.3.167–8; II.4.21–4; III.2.61–2, 71–4, 81–2, 102–3, 119–20, 184–93, 210–18; III.3.70–1, 131–2, 174–5, 194–5, 207–9; III.4.27–8, 65–6, 90–1, 100–7; IV.1.148–9, 187–98, 200–1, 219–20, 316–17, 321–4, 332–3; V.1.24–5, 79–82, 85–102; V.2.39–40, 50–1; V.3.33–4, 48–9, 69–72, 74–135, 141–5; V.4.10–11; V.6.7–12, 17–18, 22–3, 28–9, 31–52

Long speeches: I.2.9–36; I.3.154–73; II.1.31–68, 163–208; II.3.112–35; III.1.1–30; III.2.4–26, 36–62, 144–77; III.3.31–61, 72–100, 143–75; IV.1.114–49, 200–20; V.5.1–66

Word-play: I.4.11–19; II.1–32, 72–99, 137–40; II.2.5–40; III.2.178–85, 210; III.3.133–41, 160–83, 200–7; III.4.12–23; IV.1.162–76, 190–201, 251–61, 289–301; V.1.86–102

Prophecies of doom: II.1.31–9, 200–8; II.2.9–12, 34–40: II.4.8–15; III.2.189; III.3.91–100; IV.1.134–49, 321–2; V.1.55–68

Divine right of kings: I.2.37–41; III.2.27–32, 36–62, 83–9, 97–101, 129–34; III.3.72–90; IV.1.114–33

Inevitability: II.2.9–13, 62–6, 144–5; III.2.218; III.3.178; III.4. 84–9; IV.1.180–9

Recurring images and ideas:
Blood: I.1.51, 98–106, 153–5, 170–3; I.2.1–3, 10–25; I.3.123–38; II.1.120–31; III.2.77–81; III.3.42–4, 93–100; IV.1.136–44; V.5.109–14; V.6.45–51

Edward III: I.1.111–22; I.2.10–25; II.1.104–8, 120–31, 171–83; II.3.98–104

Youth/age/time: I.3.209–32; II.1.69–92, 132–4, 191–7; II.2.80–5; II.3.41–4, 98–104; V.2.88–111; V.3.1–22; V.5.41–61

Death/grave: I.1.178–81; II.1.5–16, 93–9, 139–40, 149–55, 270–1; III.2.144–85; V.1.38–50

Sun: II.4.18–22; III.2.36–55, 218; III.3.62–7; IV.1.259–61; V.2.46–51

Garden: II.1.42, 50; III.2.4–26; III.3.47; III.4; V.2.46–51

Tears/grief: I.3.253–303; I.2.54–74; II.1.184–5; II.2.1–40, 62–72, 77–9, 99–100; III.2.93–103, 204–14; III.3.133–75; IV.1.180–201, 275–301, 330–4; V.1.1–50, 81–102; V.2.30–6; V.5.1–66; V.6.38–52

Words/tongue/breath: I.1.47–50, 190–5; I.3.159–73, 213–5, 243–6; I.4.11–19; II.1.228–9, 1–32, 84–92; III.2.156; III.3.133–6; IV.1.273–4, 327–8; V.1.40–50, 93–102; V.2.1–3, 23–9; V.3.78–82, 99–103; V.5.97

A student will want to be well-informed, but once he has done all he can to master the nature of the text, he should trust to his own responses. Literary discussion is not a science. Certainly, we can carefully scrutinise and describe features of the text, but our final verdict is not a scientific fact but a matter of personal appreciation. Literary discussion is mere mimicry if we only repeat what others have said about a text. We should always try to read the opinions of others *critically*, and decide for ourselves whether we agree with them or not (and that certainly includes the reading of these Notes). We should try to be honest with ourselves, and give our own ideas about a text. It is not easy to be honest; it is much easier simply to do what we have been told, to follow others. But it is by trying to understand our *own* feelings as we read that we ourselves grow, as our knowledge of literature grows. And, furthermore, it is personal commitment and insight which enlivens essays and marks them out as the work of an individual and sensitive mind.

Specimen answers

Analyse Shakespeare's presentation of any turning point in the play, and discuss its significance in the play as a whole.

Richard II is a play with a single plot and a simple structure. It focuses clearly upon Richard's decline and Henry's rise to power. Nothing distracts our attention from this movement, which proceeds in four clear stages. First we meet Richard in his full regal splendour, but various hints that he is not the king he seems to be are developed until, by the end of II.1, we realise he is in many ways a negligent and tyrannical ruler. Richard then leaves for his Irish campaign, and in the second part of the play we watch Henry's steady progress across England, gathering support and overcoming opposition with remarkable ease. By the time of Richard's return from Ireland and the beginning of the third part of the play (III.2), we know his position is desperate: his flatterers and followers have deserted him and been executed by Henry; his Welsh army has disbanded; York has joined Henry; both the general populace and the nobles have sided with Henry. In III.2, the turning point of the play, we see the effect news of these events has upon Richard. By the end of this scene, he has abandoned all hope, and we know Henry's success is assured. What follows is but the inevitable transference of power, followed in its turn, in the final part of the play, by the rule of Henry. Thus, although a number of other scenes stand out as turning points (Richard's seizure of Henry's inheritance in II.1, for example, or the deposition scene in IV.1), we have a pivotal point in III.2 upon which the whole action turns.

The scene begins in an ironical mood for, having returned from Ireland, Richard is in an optimistic frame of mind, idealistically (and impractically) confident that his mere kingly presence will be sufficient to win support and shame the rebels into submission. We, however, have seen in Act II the balance of power shift decisively to Henry and know that matters are much more serious than Richard realises. During the scene he comes to learn what the audience already knows, the true state of things. As he does so, our knowledge of *him* is greatly increased. Shakespeare has chosen to focus the scene on Richard's reactions to a succession of tidings about what has happened during his absence. This marks the beginning of Shakespeare's concentration of the play upon Richard and his feelings, and so enables us to come to know him more intimately and appreciatively than we have done hitherto. In particular, we learn that he is capable of extraordinarily expressive poetry, that he is emotionally unstable, and that, while he is quite incapable of acting resolutely as a leader of men, he has a nature of great sensitivity. Taken together, these features humanise Richard, so that, the extravagant and negligent king of the early scenes now largely forgotten, we respond to him with a new sympathy as we watch him in adversity.

The scene follows Richard as he see-saws between hope and despair. As he lands at Barkloughly, he is overjoyed to be back in his kingdom. He conjures the earth itself to help him against the rebels in a speech which assumes the world of nature will side with the true king. It is an affecting speech, but as Richard's followers immediately point out, not much to the purpose. Richard has never been able to appreciate that even an anointed king has need to plan his actions and assess their consequences. He banished Henry, seized his inheritance and used blank charters, blissfully unaware (despite the warnings of Gaunt and York) that these deeds did not go unnoticed. So now the Bishop of Carlisle (Richard's noblest follower), while he agrees that God can indeed keep

Richard king, yet warns that men must take steps to help themselves. Aumerle stresses the point, claiming that it is their own negligence which has enabled Henry to achieve so much. Richard's reply illustrates both his nobility and his folly. He rejects this advice as unworthy of a king: he has no need of policy; like the sun itself, kingly light can shame evil. He is at once grandly idealistic and confident, and hopelessly arrogant and misguided as to his true power. Kingship in itself has little hold over men unless the man who is king deserves loyalty. This Richard has never grasped. His speech concludes 'Then if angels fight,/Weak men must fall'. The lines are sadly ironic: weak men shall fall, but not those Richard has in mind. Nor are we as sure as he which side the angels are on.

Then the first blow falls. Salisbury comes and tells Richard his Welsh army has disbanded. Immediately, Richard's optimism vanishes, but, just as suddenly, his hopes revive when Aumerle reminds him that he is still king. This is to be the pattern of the scene, and we begin to see how unsuitable a man to be king Richard is. He feels everything intensely and personally, and so is incapable of sustained effort. Thus, when Scroop arrives and tells that the entire kingdom has gone over to Henry and that Richard's favourites 'have made peace' with Henry, Richard flares up in anger, accusing them of being Judases. When he learns that they have in fact been executed by Henry, there is no word of remorse for his unjust accusation, only a despair blacker than that before. In the famous lines 'Of comfort no man speak' we have one of those speeches which, though ostensibly addressed to the other people on the stage, actually has the private and introspective quality of a soliloquy. It is by this means that Shakespeare reveals Richard's feelings to us: Richard himself analyses and reflects on them. Now he is haunted by the prospect of death and the futility of kingly splendour. He speaks as though he has already lost the crown, and we realise he will achieve Henry's success for him. However, once again he revives when reminded that there is still York and his army.

We, of course, know there is neither, and Scroop miserably admits that York has joined Henry. This is too much for Richard. He now embraces despair as though it is the realistic and creditable thing to do. Refusing to pause to consider possible plans of action, he discharges his followers, abandons the contest, and retires to Flint Castle to 'pine away'. For this man, when people no longer treat him as king, there is nothing else to do.

Thus, two things, seemingly contradictory, have happened to us in the course of this scene. On the one hand, we are now finally persuaded Richard is not made to be king. Lest we should have been in any doubt, Shakespeare has already shown us the quiet confidence and efficient organisation of Henry. There is a man with the stuff of a ruler in him. By comparison, Richard here behaves like a petulant and spoilt child, reduced to tears when someone takes his toys from him. And yet, that version of the scene ignores the poetry. The second thing that happens is that we now feel for Richard as we never did when he was unchallenged king. We are now interested in, and affected by, him because of the detailed poetic exploration of his feelings which makes up the body of the scene. In other words, Shakespeare is now turning Richard into a tragic hero: a man flawed, but sympathetic. And with the end of this scene, we are in no doubt this *is* to be a tragedy. Ironically, the final line applies to Henry the imagery of sun and light associated with the King: 'From Richard's night to Bolingbroke's fair day'.

Analyse Gaunt's speech in II.1.31–68. Assess the effectiveness of the significant features of the speech through your analysis and relate the speech to the wider concerns of the play.

Richard II pays little attention to the political intrigues and military actions which are usually the main concerns of Elizabethan history plays. Shakespeare seems to be more interested in people's reactions to events rather than in the events themselves. Hence, the main scenes of the play are scenes in which people discuss and analyse the thoughts and feelings which circumstances have provoked in them. In III.2, for example, Richard returns from Ireland and the entire scene is made up of his reactions to the news of Henry's successful invasion. This emphasis means there are many long speeches in the play. Although only one of them (Richard's meditation in Pomfret Castle in V.5) is properly a soliloquy, many of them have the private and reflective quality we associate with soliloquies. These tend to make great use of metaphor (Richard actually begins his soliloquy in V.5 by calling attention to this technique) and to follow a mind as it moves, not through a logical argument, but from one idea to the next. Gaunt's speech in II.1 is of this kind.

Gaunt is dying, and is awaiting the King, who, we know from I.4, is coming in an unsympathetic mood. Gaunt has hopes that at last his warnings about the consequences of the King's behaviour will have some effect, but his brother York is of the opinion that Gaunt will be but wasting his breath. It is with word-play on breathing in ('inspire') and out ('expire') that the speech begins. The idea that dying men enjoyed a moment of extraordinary insight was common. Shakespeare gives it added point here in the compression of these lines. Gaunt has a vision breathed into him by God, which he now, like a prophet, breathes out as he speaks and as he literally expires (dies). This opening alerts us to the oracular nature of what is to follow and prepares us to listen to his words with great seriousness.

The following lines contain the first of many prophecies in the play that Richard cannot go on as he is without dire consequences resulting. The images stress the brevity of things bright and violent (lightning, fire, storm). They aptly reflect both the splendour of Richard's reign and its underlying cruelty (of which we have had an example in Gloucester's murder). Gaunt then introduces the idea of over-indulgence and extravagance. Like the cormorant, Richard will destroy himself. The lines are a succinct summary of (and prepare us for) the course of Richard's final years as king.

Then the speech assumes the quality of a vision. Gaunt moves from the particular failings of Richard to the prospect of the England which Richard so neglects and misrules. It is Gaunt's patriotic dedication to England which is the source of his anxiety at Richard's behaviour and which spurs him on to make one last effort to reform the King with his dying words. In Gaunt's mind, England is a place especially favoured both by nature and by God. It is, as a fertile island, both prosperous and protected from enemies and evil foreign influences (the Elizabethan audience would remember how, only seven years ago, the English Channel had prevented the success of the Spanish Armada). And it seems God has bestowed on this island special grace. This is conveyed by the images of paradise ('Eden') and jewels ('precious stone') and culminates in the phrase 'blessed plot'. Running through these images are those conveying its natural advantages: the 'fortress' built by 'nature', the 'wall' and the 'moat'. The speech moves to the climax of 'this England', by which time we have received an impression of it as a self-contained world ('little world') which enjoys all the blessings and lacks all the blemishes of the larger world beyond the sea.

Gaunt goes on to admire the people, and especially the royal and noble people, of this island. The 'happy breed of men' he had mentioned earlier are seen as literally the children of England ('this teeming womb'). This suggests that the peculiarly favourable conditions of England produce men rarely endowed. Gaunt concentrates upon the achievements of the English in crusades, and likens the extent of their reputation to that of the scene of the resurrection of Christ. This comparison both exalts the English and continues the religious thread in the speech. These are Christian knights, as befits the people of 'Eden'.

The movement of this part of the speech reaches a climax in the repeated 'dear', an example of Shakespeare making fruitful use of the pun. The word captures both Gaunt's affection for this land (it is dear to him) and its value (it is of high estimation in the various ways Gaunt has mentioned). It is at this moment of climax that the speech abruptly changes direction. Here we see Shakespeare following the actual working of a mind. At the very moment that Gaunt is wrapt in his contemplation of England he remembers the shame she now endures under Richard, and the contrast is such that he breaks out in anger at the illegal practices of the King. We know from I.4 that the charges are only too true. And so the sea which earlier had been a defensive wall against the outside world becomes now a prison wall shutting in England's shame. England, unassailable from without, has conquered itself from within. The conquest Gaunt has in mind is, of course, a moral, not a military, one. This is consistent with the religious tenor of his earlier remarks.

Thus, the speech does several things. It conveys to us the patriotic devotion of this old, experienced nobleman. Our estimation of Gaunt is enhanced considerably by it. This in turn makes his criticisms of Richard the more compelling. As he says it, we feel Richard has behaved shamefully. We are firmly on Gaunt's side in the quarrel which follows soon after this speech when Richard enters. Furthermore, now Gaunt has awakened in us a love of England, we respond more deeply to Richard's neglect of the land. Above all, the speech has created in our minds a vision of England which will linger throughout the play. Indeed, Shakespeare has here expressed not only the particular feelings of one character in a play, nor even only the patriotic pride of his fellow Elizabethans: he has caught and expressed the devotion to their country of Englishmen of all ages.

Part 5

Suggestions for further reading

The text

WELLS, S. (ED.): *Richard II*, (The New Penguin Shakespeare) Penguin Books, Harmondsworth, 1969. This has a very helpful introduction and excellent detailed notes in the commentary which follows the text.

MUIR, K. (ED.): *The Tragedy of King Richard II*, (The Signet Classic Shakespeare) New English Library, London, 1963. This has a useful general introduction to Shakespeare, an introductory essay to the play and glosses on the same page as the text. There is no commentary on the text, but there are helpful excerpts from critical studies of the play, a discussion of the text and sources, and long passages from the relevant sections of Holinshed.

DOVER WILSON, J. (ED.): *King Richard II*, (The New Cambridge Shakespeare) revised edition, Cambridge University Press, Cambridge, 1951. This scholarly edition has a readable introduction, a full discussion of the text, a stage history of the play, a passage from Daniel's poem and a glossary, but its notes have been superseded by Ure's edition. It has now been replaced by Andrew Gurr's edition, Cambridge, 1984.

URE, P. (ED.): *King Richard II*, (The Arden Shakespeare) fifth edition, Methuen, London, 1961; revised edition 1966. The standard scholarly edition of the play. This is an invaluable edition, but designed for the mature reader of Shakespeare.

Sources of *Richard II*

ARMSTRONG, W. A. (ED.): *Elizabethan History Plays*, (The World's Classics) Oxford University Press, London, 1965. Prints the complete text of *Thomas of Woodstock*.

BULLOUGH, G. (ED.): *Narrative and Dramatic Sources of Shakespeare*, seven vols, Routledge, London, 1957–75, vol III. Reprints passages from Hall, Holinshed, *A Mirror for Magistrates*, Froissart, the *Chronique de la Traison*, Daniel's poem, and *Woodstock*, with an admirable introductory essay on Shakespeare's use of his sources.

HOLDERNESS, GRAHAM: *Shakespeare's History*, Gill & Macmillan, Dublin and New York, 1985.

NICOLL, A. and J. (EDS): *Holinshed's Chronicle as used in Shakespeare's Plays*, (Everyman's Library) Dent, London, 1927. Reprints relevant passages from Holinshed.

General works on Shakespeare

ALEXANDER, P.: *Shakespeare*, (Home University Library) Oxford University Press, Oxford, 1964. A sound introduction to Shakespeare's life and work.

BAYLEY, PETER: *An A·B·C of Shakespeare*, (Longman York Handbooks) Longman, Harlow, 1985. New edition, 1993.

BRADBROOK, M. C.: *The Rise of the Common Player: A Study of Actor and Society in Shakespeare's England*, Chatto, London, 1967; reissued Cambridge University Press, Cambridge, 1979.

GURR, A.: *Playgoing in Shakespeare's London*, Cambridge University Press, Cambridge, 1987.

HALLIDAY, F. E.: *A Shakespeare Companion 1564–1964*, Penguin Books, Harmondsworth, 1964. An encyclopaedia of Shakespeare: alphabetically arranged entries cover nearly everything to do with Shakespeare's life, times, theatre and plays.

MUIR, K. and SCHOENBAUM, S. (EDS): *A New Companion to Shakespeare Studies*, Cambridge University Press, Cambridge, 1971. A collection of essays by different scholars covering such things as Shakespeare's life, the Elizabethan theatre, Shakespeare's English, and his social and historical background.

ONIONS, C. T.: *A Shakespeare Glossary*, second edition, Clarendon Press, Oxford, 1958, revised by Robert D. Eagleson, Oxford, 1986. A dictionary of Shakespeare's English, which explains the meanings of all words either not now in use or used in a different sense.

SCHOENBAUM, S.: *William Shakespeare: A Compact Documentary Life*, Clarendon Press, Oxford, 1977; paperback 1978. The most recent and authoritative biography.

Studies of *Richard II* and Shakespeare's history plays

ARMSTRONG, W. A. (ED.): *Shakespeare's Histories: An Anthology of Modern Criticism*, (Penguin Shakespeare Library) Penguin Books, Harmondsworth, 1972.

BROOKE, N. (ED.): *Richard II: A Casebook*, Macmillan, London, 1973. A collection of passages on the play which includes extracts from all the major studies of it.

BROOKE, N.: *Shakespeare's Early Tragedies*, Methuen, London, 1968.

BROWN, J. R. and HARRIS, B. (EDS): *Early Shakespeare*, (Stratford-upon-Avon Studies 3) Edward Arnold, London, 1961. Includes a lucid study of rhetoric in the play by R. F. Hill.

CAMPBELL, LILY: *Shakespeare's 'Histories': Mirrors of Elizabethan Policy*, The Huntington Library, San Marino, 1947. This study discusses the relevance to contemporary Elizabethan politics of the ideas in the plays; a valuable, but not an introductory, book.

HUMPHREYS, A. R.: *Richard II*, (Arnold's Studies in English Literature 31), Edward Arnold, London, 1967. An extremely helpful introductory critical guide to the play.

KNIGHT, G. WILSON: *The Imperial Theme*, Methuen, London, 1951; University Paperbacks, Routledge, London 1989.

KNIGHTS, L. C.: *Shakespeare: The Histories*, Longman, for the British Council, London, 1962.

MACK, M., JR: *Killing the King*, (Yale Studies in English 180) Yale University Press, New Haven, 1973. Includes a sympathetic study of Richard.

MAHOOD, M. M.: *Shakespeare's Wordplay*, Methuen, London, 1957; paperback, 1979. A chapter on *Richard II* comments on the language of the play.

PALMER, J.: *Political Characters of Shakespeare*, Macmillan, London, 1945. Includes a very perceptive study of Richard.

REESE, M. M.: *The Cease of Majesty: A Study of Shakespeare's History Plays*, Edward Arnold, London, 1961. Shows that Shakespeare was actively engaged in examining ideas of majesty and duty in the history plays; has valuable comments on Richard's notion of the divine right of kings.

ROSSITER, A. P.: *Angel with Horns: Fifteen Lectures*, edited by Graham Storey, Longman, Harlow, 1989 (paperback).

TILLYARD, E. M. W.: *Shakespeare's History Plays*, Chatto and Windus, London, 1944. This study of Elizabethan views of history, the Elizabethan view of the fifteenth century, the literary background to the plays can be wholeheartedly recommended.

TRAVERSI, D.: *Shakespeare: From Richard II to Henry V*, Hollis and Carter, London, 1958. The chapter on *Richard II* follows the course of the play and is enlightened on the earlier scenes and the character of Henry.

The author of these notes

N.H. KEEBLE was educated at St David's College, Lampeter, and the University of Oxford. He was a Lecturer in English Literature at the University of Aarhus, Denmark, before taking up his present position as Lecturer in English at the University of Stirling in Scotland. He has edited Richard Baxter's *Autobiography* for Dent's Everyman University Library Series (1974), and John Bunyan's *The Pilgrim's Progress* for Oxford's World's Classics series (1984). He is also the author of *Richard Baxter: Puritan Man of Letters* (Clarendon Press, Oxford, 1982) as well as a number of articles on late medieval and Renaissance literature.